How to Make
White People Laugh

How to Make White People Laugh

NEGIN FARSAD

GRAND CENTRAL
PUBLISHING

NEW YORK   BOSTON

Grand Central Publishing
Hachette Book Group
1290 Avenue of the Americas
New York, NY 10104

www.HachetteBookGroup.com

Printed in the United States of America

RRD-C

First Edition: May 2016

10 9 8 7 6 5 4 3 2 1

Grand Central Publishing is a division of Hachette Book Group, Inc.
The Grand Central Publishing name and logo is a trademark of Hachette Book Group, Inc.

The Hachette Speakers Bureau provides a wide range of authors for speaking events. To find out more, go to www.hachettespeakersbureau.com or call (866) 376-6591.

The publisher is not responsible for websites (or their content) that are not owned by the publisher.

Library of Congress Cataloging-in-Publication Data

Names: Farsad, Negin, author.
Title: How to make white people laugh / by Negin Farsad.
Description: First edition. | New York : Grand Central Publishing, 2016.
Identifiers: LCCN 2016001565 | ISBN 9781455558223 (hardback) | ISBN 9781478908685 (audio download) | ISBN 9781455558209 (ebook)
Subjects: LCSH: Farsad, Negin. | Women comedians—United States—Biography. |
BISAC: BIOGRAPHY & AUTOBIOGRAPHY / Personal Memoirs.
Classification: LCC PN2287.F3525 A3 2016 | DDC 792.702/8092—dc23 LC record available at http://lccn.loc.gov/2016001565
ISBN: 978-1-45555-822-3

To My Parents who gave me America

Contents

Chapter 9: My Own People Don't Like Me

How to Make
White People Laugh

AN INTRODUCTION:
I USED TO BE BLACK

Like most comedians, I have a graduate degree in African-American Studies.

To be clear, I'm actually an Iranian-American Muslim female comedian-slash-filmmaker. (I thought of making that description longer by adding "honey mustard enthusiast," but I'm trying to exercise what my publishers call editorial discretion, which supposedly means "don't add every stupid descriptor that pops into your head." Sorry, I didn't mean to get too technical.)

Here's the thing: I used to feel black. Sometimes "kinda pretty black," occasionally "really black," and, depending on how drunk I was, "Don Cheadle." I'm not technically black. Or even on the black spectrum. I'm Iranian, an ethnically brown Muz type, and definitely not black. Further evidence of not being black: I can't play basketball or U.S. President *at all*.

NEGIN'S FEELING SPECTRUM

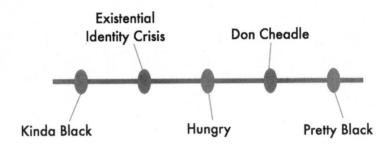

Existential
Identity Crisis   Don Cheadle

Kinda Black   Hungry   Pretty Black

There's probably a seventeen-year-old living in Cedar
Rapids, Iowa, who knows exactly what I mean when I say
"feeling black." But for the rest of you, let me explain.

. You could identify blackness by external appearance. I
fail on that count. You know, because I'm not black. You
could define it based on the one-drop rule, which is to say
if you have any black ancestry, however remote, you're
black. I fail on this count, too. I've never done a family
tree and I've never been the subject of one of those reality TV shows where they trace the family history of say,
Ben Affleck, and he finds out that he and Matt Damon
are connected eight generations back through a soldier
in the Revolutionary War who wore custom pantaloons.
I'm pretty sure my ancestors are Persian. An Arab dude
probably came in and had his way with a Persian lady
somewhere in there, but I don't know where that dude
was before he boned the Persian or anything about *his*
family. So, I don't rate on the one-drop rule, either. Basi-

cally, external appearance and *CSI*-style blood forensics don't get me closer to blackness.

But then there's the kind of blackness that's defined by its opposition to *whiteness*. It's the binary we've all been living with. The Civil Rights movement was driven by black folk *against* white folk who were trying to keep them down. Slavery was black folks being *owned* by white folks. The race question in the United States since the beginning of its inception has been Black in Relation to White. Everything in the U.S. is black and white, ebony and ivory, Black Eyed Peas and White Stripes. But what if you don't fit in this binary?

I guess what I'm saying is, I felt black in that I wasn't white. My definition of blackness was never about the externalities, it was about the gooey, inexplicable internalities.[1] Growing up with immigrant parents, I felt like my minority and ethnic status was the flashpoint of national blame for some kind of social tension, but I didn't exactly know what or why or how. I felt like I was or should have been involved in *the* struggle, but the only nationally recognized struggle was (and basically still is) the black struggle. So my still burgeoning mind decided to embrace the struggle, embrace that blackness. It was the only narrative around "otherness" out there. Blackness had TV shows and books. It had everything from *Roots* to Cornel West. And somewhere in between: *A Different World*. Come on! That shit was hot. It meant something,

---

1. And just to be clear, I was never "Dolezaling"—I was never trying to pass or pretend or mask—it was never like that.

it was easy to understand. It represented the struggle in a pleasing and easy-to-swallow sitcom! Dwayne Wayne had flip-up glasses!

So I felt the blackness and I applied to Columbia University's Graduate School of Arts and Sciences for a degree in African-American Studies and, miraculously, I was accepted. On my first day, I discovered I was the only nonblack person in the program. I was pretty stunned by this—didn't other nonblack people feel as outsidery as I did? Wasn't there one other nonblack-ethnic-diasporic-whatchamacallit in the whole City of New York who identified with the black struggle in their bones and wanted to formalize the feeling with a master's degree? To that question, the City of New York said, "No, not that we know of," then offered me another slice of pizza and an opportunity to yell at a cabbie for pedestrian-unfriendly behavior.

The program itself was exhilarating and for those of you who know black celebrity scholars, I got to work with *the* Manning Marable. Marable was like the Meryl Streep of black scholarship. He was great in a way that no one questioned... and he never seemed to age. RIP, Marable, no one could ever whip up an analysis of the economic underdevelopment of the black community vis-à-vis modern capitalism like you could. You were dreamy.

But as you can imagine, there's only so many critiques of Orientalism or Marxist reinterpretations of Malcolm X that a gal like me could read before she wondered how it all applied to the real world. Enter former New York City mayor David Dinkins. *Hold up! You're saying that a former New York City mayor figured into your life?* Yeah, motherfuckers, deal with it, I have a personal connection with David Dinkins, the first (and only) black mayor of New York. Now, would David Dinkins remember me? Totally. Maybe. Probably maybe. Okay, not really.

Dinkins is by far my favorite New York City mayor whose leadership I never got to experience firsthand. (Warning, Dinkins shout-out coming up.) He taught a great class on how to run cities, for which he was extraqualified because he ran one. It was Dinkins—not Rudy Giuliani—who started the Times Square cleanup and built up the police force to the point where it could reduce crime. Yeah, I've always been bitter that Giuliani gets credited with bringing crime reduction and order to NYC, because it was Dinkins! But is Dinkins bitter? No. Because he's one of those nonpetty rise-above-it type people. (I'm one of those "write an angry paragraph trying to correct history" type people.)

Dinkins taught a class at Columbia's School of International and Public Affairs, where policy wonks get their schoolin'. I was hooked. And I decided to get a dual master's degree in public policy, where I would learn the nuts and bolts of administering and changing cities, states, and countries. At the same time, over in the African-American Studies department, I would learn all the theoretical underpinnings of why I would do what I wanted to do. I interned for the likes of Rep. Charles Rangel (D-NY) and the Campaign Finance Board. I was graduate-educating real hard.[2]

---

2. Two masters degrees is a must-have for any comedian.

Back then I wasn't going to be a comedian, I was going to be the first Muslim president (but Obama beat me to it).[3] My calling was to end the racial divide. I was a part of the struggle—the only struggle that had things like leaders, legitimate entities, graduate programs, mainstream recognition, and pop stars. I felt so totally committed, so totally in the thick of blackness. *That* struggle didn't include any Iranians, but at the time I thought, Close enough. That's what a lot of hyphenated Americans say to themselves when they glom onto the larger minority groups: close enough.

It felt good, it felt like I was finally a part of the fight! It's comforting to be surrounded by a group that *basically* knows what you mean even if they don't *exactly* know what you mean. I would start sentences with "In Harlem we...." I lived in Queens, so I didn't quite know what happened in Harlem, but I was in the African-American studies program at Columbia, which was...Harlem adjacent. So that wasn't horribly untrue, was it? (It was.)

But I should note that I went to grad school in the aftermath of 9/11. That event sparked a little something we now like to call Islamophobia. I thought this little spike in Muz-hate was going to dissipate quickly. How naïve. I really thought, how could people associate this

---

3. Come on! Obama is not Muslim....Probably. He isn't. No really. I'm almost sure he isn't.*
*Oh yeah, footnotes—it's *that* kind of book.

kind of violence with a whole religion (Islam) and an entire region (the Middle East)—that's just crazy! That's like stereotyping 1.6 billion people. Who does that? Americans. We Americans do that. Post 9/11, mainstream American media was all about creating the following critical associations:

> **Islam** = the promotion of violence.
> **Muslims** = violent people with dusty faces always running around the desert.
> **The Middle East** = a place full of violent people with dusty faces always running around the desert, plus women shrouded in what appear to be blankets.

But it's not like Muslims were so totally adored before 9/11. When my parents moved to Virginia during the Iran Hostage Crisis, my brother would get beaten up in school for being Iranian. We lived in Virginia until I was seven years old, and I remember in kindergarten a girl yelled at me for being "a communist." How embarrassing for her: She had the political regime all wrong! I came back with the very clever retort, "You mean Islamic Republic." And that's about as much as either of us could say on geopolitics. But for five-year-olds, that was pretty good.

After the hostage crisis, Muslims kinda went on the back burner. Americans got real busy hating on Russians. But not too busy for the classic hating on black people. Then we had Mexicans to worry about, gotta save some hate for them. Plus all those Asians who apparently drive badly...oh, bigotry had a busy schedule! But 9/11 changed the national discourse by giving America a brand-new enemy.

I was in grad school, hard at work being politically black—preaching the words of Medgar Evers and Malcolm X. I memorized an argument on the critical race theory underpinning of *The Fresh Prince of Bel-Air*. I was prepared to change my name to "Tyler Perry Presents Negin Farsad." I was ready to fight for black causes whenever and wherever!

My classmates were sorta like, "Um, yeah, could you stop doing that? It's weird." Didn't I have my own people to fight for?

And that's when it struck me: I wasn't black, or Mexican or Asian or Russian. I was an Iranian-American Muslim female (the comedy, filmmaking, and honey-mustard enthusiasm didn't come till later). To large swaths of the American public, that meant I was a possibly dangerous brown person who potentially sympathized with Al Qaeda or Hezbollah. To other swaths of the American public, I was the kind of person who pronounced "Iran" in a way that didn't make it sound like a past-tense verb.

I needed to come out of the closet. I wasn't helping anyone by glossing over my real identity. *This* was my struggle, and I had work to do! There were 1.6 billion Muslims worldwide whose identity was being hijacked! People needed to know that secular, fun Muslims who smell nice are the norm—more the norm than the dusty brown people we were seeing on television. And I had to let people know it with the only tool I had: comedy. (Actually, I also had one of those little wrenches that came with the IKEA Fjälkinge shelf, but I didn't think I could take on bigotry with that.)

Even though I went to graduate school for African American Studies and public policy (not at all for comedy) and even though I didn't know it at the time, graduate school was preparing me for this work. Getting that education made me realize how little time we all spent exploring other minority groups. It made me realize that the hyphenates were getting the short end of the stick, and that the stick we did get was from a really old twig that had already served its time as a snowman's right hand. I also figured out that if you want to broaden and tackle the issue of race relations with jokes, I guess it's not bad to have an academic foundation in race relations. I could have lived without the debt, though, 'cause that shit was expensive. My plan was to reverse the iconography that stemmed from all the bigotry, xenophobia, and general shittiness with something I call *social justice comedy*.

The characters we see on TV, those shows, they become iconic representations, and iconic representations are limiting. They define things. They're sticky, like when you get superglue on your fingers and it takes three days of excessive scrubbing to get it off. Except three days in this case is more like several decades, and the superglue is possibly something really awful, like a stereotype that results in bigotry.

Stay with me here, as I am about say something that

makes it sound like I went to grad school. What follows is what you might call a theoretical argument. Or a bunch of images with blurbs next to them—your choice.

What Are Iconic Representations?

I breezily mentioned icons above, but let's not get ahead of ourselves, let's first talk about what icons are! Let's look at some examples that'll go down real smooth. For example, when I was growing up, if you said the word *dancer*, I thought of these ladies:[4]

4. An image from the Metropolitan Museum archives by some famous artist.

I didn't necessarily think of these ladies:

To me, a dancer was a be-tutu'd, rail-thin girl who might or might not have an eating disorder. The iconic dancer does ballet or, at worst, ballroom dancing. She doesn't pop, lock, drop, shake, strobe, grind, krump, or twerk. Though she may do Zumba. The iconic definition of a dancer for me is simply not correlated with this kind of *booty overload*.

What do you think of when you hear the word *artist*? I think of this kind of dude:

He's got the Flock of Seagulls haircut. He's wearing a smock, he's standing next to an easel, he's wielding a paintbrush, he's got an asshole-ishness to him. His work is esteemed, it's shown in highfalutin museums and galleries. The dude just screams *artist*!

But this dude—a guy I like to call Oscar Wilde, because that was his name—is also technically an "artist":

Oh yes, Oscar rocked a fur coat *and* a scepter. He gave everyone a run for their money by being hilarious, unconventional, and smart at the same time. When they found out he was gay, well...Throw this man into prison, they said! And they did.

And weirdly, this guy is also an "artist":

This image butts against the iconic understanding of "artist," because she appears to be a stand-up comic making fart noises with her face.[5] What's confounding this stereotype even more is that this stand-up comic is a woman. *Weird.*

If you think representations of artists have been limiting, think about the plight of fruit. Fruit have been depicted in bowls from the beginning of icons itself.

Fruit in a bowl in the eighteenth century:

Fruit in a bowl in the seventeenth century:

5. The "she" in this case is "me," because that's a picture of me. As I write this, I am also making fart noises with my face.

Holy hot pants, this is fruit in a bowl in the first century BC!! Like forever ago:

Little known French artist Paul Cézanne tried to depict fruit *outside* of bowls:

For this violation of fruit iconography, Cézanne was beheaded.[6] All of this to say that these kinds of representations really stick.

When Ethnic and Religious Iconography Turn to Crap

So icons are limiting and they also have a tendency of creating monolithic definitions of large groups of people. Since I'm a Middle Eastern lady Muz, why don't I share some of my people's chart-topping iconic faves?

1. Women shrouded in black sheets with slits at the eyeball area.

Photo by Steve Evans

For your eyes only

---

6. This isn't true, but it's one of those things that could almost be true because it was the 1800s, and at that time in France they beheaded people for the most hilarious reasons. Just before that, in the late 1700s the guillotine was so popular that it was made into a child's toy so that kids could decapitate their dolls. I know, so cute.

This icon does a good job of making the entire Middle East seem really medieval. A place where women have no rights and they probably don't even realize they're missing rights because it's like 1320 (or whatever year they're peddling) over there. There's no way they could actually *want* to cover themselves! And what? Miss out on all the great catcalling from construction workers? No way!

This icon also does a great job of suggesting that there are no separate countries in the Middle East—it's just one big brown violent blob where women float through fake borders in their black sheets as if hovering over the sandy deserts, defying gravity. I mean, never mind the fact that burkas are mostly a Saudi thing or that in Beirut ladies are more likely to look like Salma Hayek bearing smoking-hot cleave.

This icon also satisfies a weird fetish, too: This mysterious Middle Eastern woman is probably naked under there, she's probably waiting for a dude to come give her sex opportunities. She's poised to pop out a tit on command!

This image says "Muslim Female in the Middle East" more than anything else, but it doesn't communicate the fact that this woman is actually in a very small minority. It doesn't communicate that women in Iran, for example, have the highest rate of degree attainment in the Middle East, outpacing that of men. Or that women in Jordan drive, or that women in Lebanon run for office. And win.

How do I know that this icon has impressed itself on the eyeballs of the American public? Well, I tour the country doing stand-up, and whenever people find out that I'm Muslim, their first question is "If you're a Muslim, why are you dressed like that?" Or they say "Are you supposed to wear

one of those things that cover your whole face and body?"
I have to deal with this question over and over again. I try
to be creative and answer in different and adventurous ways
but ugh…sometimes I just wish people knew. Maybe if this
icon wasn't so pervasive, people *would know*.

2. Dusty dudes hanging out in desert-like situations
with beards and weapons.

A bearded affair

Seriously, for real, Middle Eastern dudes like to chill
outdoors with their weapons! Not only that, they do
it while having very hot-faced beards. What a simultaneously violent and hairy icon! You know what else—
when these guys aren't taking a little shaded rest with
their weapons, they're running in formation with their
weapons. When they're not doing that, they're probably
cleaning their weapons. You know how there's always a

"falling in love" montage in a romantic comedy? That's basically what the life of a Middle Eastern dude is, except it's a three-way with his weapon and his beard. It's basically the dude, the weapon, and the beard in the meadows. The dude, the weapon, and the beard eating ice cream together. The dude, the weapon, and the beard getting buck naked and boning.

Question
The cast of *Duck Dynasty*: Muslim, Amish, or other?

Answer
I know what you're thinking: Every man on that show has a beard and runs around with guns so, total Muz. But, the patriarch on the show, Phil Robertson, dislikes technology and doesn't own a cell phone, which puts him squarely in the Amish camp. But the answer is: other! *Ding ding!* (The family belongs to the White's Ferry Road Church of Christ, wherein homosexuality is a sin.)

I'm not saying that there aren't Middle Eastern men who are weapon-and-beard based. Of course there are! But again, that's a minority. The proportion of bearded dudes with weapons in the Middle East is probably the same as bearded dudes with weapons in the United States. It should also be noted that we would probably have more bearded dudes in the U.S. but we don't, because some guys grow patchy beards, so it doesn't really make sense for them to have beards at all. But they should be counted because they *would* have beards if their faces let them.

This isn't the first time that we've depicted men of a certain racial and ethnic background as violent. We've done it to African-American men, too, presenting them in mass media imagery as savage brutes. That shit goes back to *Birth of a Nation* in 1915.[7] What's that thing about repeating mistakes? Fool me once, shame on you, fool me twice, shame another group with the savage brute imagery? Maybe it's easier to wage large-scale wars in the Middle East if the people you're killing are seen as animal-istic. Because if we replace the weapon with a guitar, these iconic Muslims would end up looking like tan American folk singers, and maybe the killing wouldn't be so easy.

3. Middle Eastern people pray their pants off.

Oh yes, the iconic image of the Muslim in prayer. Holy shit, how much do brown people pray? I mean, really?

---

7. Hell yeah, I can reference a really old movie from the canon of cinema. I went to college!

What's worse is, it's that really intense praying where they have to get up and down and kneel and bow—it's almost like a CrossFit workout—and every time there's a news story involving Muslims, that CrossFit-praying-Muslim image is streaming on a bunch of different channels. It plays so much that it seems like Middle Easterners *just constantly pray.*

Photo by Antonio Melina/Agência Brasil

This kind of imagery leads people to think that all of us Middle Easterners are hardcore, practicing Muslims. And what's the stereotype of hardcore, practicing people of any religion? They're the zealot-nutjobby ones. In the case of Muslims, *praying = nutjob.*

Contrast this to the image of, let's say, a Christian, kneeling with their hands in prayer position at their heart. Are they considered nutjobs or pure-of-heart-jobs?

You've probably watched a scene in a movie where

a little girl prays with her dad? Picture it, there's that moment where the dad and the little girl are barricaded in the little girl's room because there are monsters outside. The monsters have already eaten most of the family, and the dad and the little girl are all that's left. Once the barricade gives out, the dad is going to have to fight the monsters. But, first, Dad and little girl have to pray! They get down on their knees, lean against a bed with a sparkly pink comforter on it, and they pray. They pray hard. It's that prayer that gets them through the next scene where the dad has to bare-knuckle-fight the monsters.

I like that scene in those movies. It makes them human. But for some reason the iconic Muslim prayer gets reduced to nutjobbery. Isn't praying supposed to be a nice thing? Isn't it supposed to help us fight the monsters?

4. Is that a nuclear weapon in your pants or are you happy to see me? Yes, actually, it *is* a nuclear weapon, because I'm Iranian and we all have one we keep in our pants.

This is more like a concept than an icon but it basically goes like this: If you're Iranian, you've been developing nuclear weapons. The thing with Iranians is that we're all enriching uranium all the time. You'll be hard-pressed to find an Iranian who *doesn't* know how to enrich uranium. In fact, I'm enriching uranium right now. It smells like bacon.

Delicious Uranium Cake

The desire for nuclear weaponry is the only reason Iranians are in the news! There's basically been a cavalcade of stories where either Iran is maybe enriching weapons-grade uranium, or they're probably totally enriching weapons-grade uranium. *Or* inspectors were in the country and they couldn't find anything but that's probably because the Iranians have figured out how to enrich *invisible* uranium. *Or* it sorta looks like Iran *could* be on the verge of having a whole bunch of atomic bombs, or the bombs are probably even pointed at every country and even though there's no real proof we should invade and get this over with.

What I like about this endless nuclear haranguing is that it implies two things: (1) Iranians are super into mass murder, the kind that comes from setting off nuclear weapons; and (2) Iranians are smart enough to *build* nuclear weapons. Oh yeah! We smart! At least this is a

IRANIANS AND ARABS, TWO DIFFERENT THINGS

Often Iranians and Arabs get lumped into the same thing. I've been called Arab a million times and I absolutely don't care. *But* I should mention for the sake of accuracy that they are technically different. Like how the French and Italian are technically different even though they both make delicious bread. Iranians and Arabs do share an alphabet (though that alphabet was imposed on the Iranians through some invasion shenanigans), and a majority of both groups are Muslim. But our languages and food are completely different. The first recorded Iranians showed up around 538 BC and the Arabs showed up around AD 835. So you know, they're different. But again, if you get it wrong, I won't be mad.

slight improvement over the "dusty dudes in the desert" icon, because those dudes seem kind of dumb. They don't look like nuclear engineers. But I would say the positives here are outweighed by the "murderous warlords with plans of global nuclear domination" thing. So it's a net loss.

And that concludes our lesson on iconic representations. See what I mean? Icons are sticky and limiting all at the same time. The ones allotted to people like me—violent, covered, and bearded—are nothing to write home about[8]... and they offend my fashion senses. This,

---

8. Although you can write a book about them, or at least devote part of a chapter to them.

my friends, is stage one—admitting there's a problem. There's a problem! Now, what are we gonna do about it?

Here's What I'm Gonna Do About It, aka Lube the Nation

There's a definitive book on race—but it's usually for black people. There's a definitive book on religion—but it's usually for Christian people. There's a definitive book on the immigrant experience—but it's usually about Ellis Island, or it's about Mexican people, or it's about Ellis Island. We seem to think those are the only groups out there! I want to give voice to the multihyphenated Americans caught in the margins. I want to give voice to all those feelings of self-censorship and cross-cultural pressure that they feel. I want mainstream American culture to take note, because we can't be ignored anymore, and recognizing us is a matter of social justice.

But here's the deal: I can give voice all I want, but that don't mean shit if I can't get through to white America. Now, I hear you saying: Why do white people matter anyway?

Because, here's the thing: White people (still) sorta control stuff. In fact, here's a handy list of things white people dominate that matter a great deal to humans. This is by no means an exhaustive list—I'm forgetting at least one to six items—but I think it's good enough to demonstrate the extent of what white people control:

- ☐ The Government
- ☐ The Economy
- ☐ Outer Space
- ☐ HBO's *Game of Thrones*
- ☐ The career of Tom Hanks
- ☐ International currency valuation
- ☐ Professional hockey
- ☐ iPhones
- ☐ The breeding of small dogs
- ☐ War
- ☐ Printer ink
- ☐ Peace
- ☐ Monogrammed towels
- ☐ Culture

I know what you're thinking: Come on, White People handle so much of this stuff so well! Why rock the boat?

Don't get me wrong, they are proficient at a lot of it. The career of Tom Hanks? I mean, how much better could that be? From *Big* to *Forrest Gump* to *Captain Phillips*, white people did *very well* with Tom. But war, for example, could use some tweaking. We have too much of it and we keep ordering more even though we know we won't ever finish it, kinda like the bottomless breadsticks at Olive Garden. And don't get me started on printer ink cartridges. Why are they so expensive, and how come they only print like four pages before they need changing again? The breeding of small dogs? None of them can ever *breathe*! That can't be right, can it?

When it comes to that last item, culture, that's where humanity is really in trouble. Culture breeds—not small dogs, but identity. Culture creates awareness around issues, it entertains and saddens, it can encourage commitment to a social contract or strengthen personal hygiene in public. Culture is *that* powerful. Culture creates the icons we follow, that we see ourselves in, that we orient ourselves toward. It's culture that tells us to love or hate, accept or tolerate, embrace or reject.

When you're a hyphenated American, you don't get a place in "culture." I'm an Iranian-American-Muslim-female-honey-mustard-enthusiast. You might be an Indo-Romanian-dumpling-fanatic or Jamaican-Irish-rum-con-noisseur (which would make you extra fun). The hyphenated types aren't represented in mainstream media. *Everybody Loves Raymond* was not about an Indian-American family living next door to naan-obsessed in-laws. *Friends* wasn't about a Filipino-American brother and sister[9] who become friends with an aspiring Czech-American actor,[10] an entrepreneurial Sri-Lankan-American,[11] and a quirky Ethiopian-Jew.[12] The television I grew up on made me aspire to, at best, Jennifer Aniston's haircut.

But I don't want Jennifer Aniston's haircut![13] I want a place in culture. I want icons. So throughout this book, I'm going to share some anecdotes from my life, some

---

9. Monica and Ross.
10. Joey.
11. Chandler.
12. Phoebe.
13. You're right, maybe I will, if the '90s look comes back in vogue.

manifestos from the trenches of social justice comedy, some unscientific charts and graphs, and hopefully only a handful of typos. The idea is that if people laugh, maybe they'll start fewer wars. Seriously. So much of our social discord comes from dominant and minority groups not getting along, not understanding each other, not lightening up! I think laughter is the key to all sorts of conflict resolution, and in these pages I want to show you how, why, where, and when this laughter is useful. I'll do that while, you know, talking about myself.

I grew up thinking, Fuck the man! but now, all I wanna do is make the man laugh! Because if you can disarm the mainstream through laughter, they're not only in store for some amazing jokes, but I daresay they're in store for some serious cultural shifts.

Protesting, lobbying, begging, yelling, lecturing, after-school special-ing—all of these things are good. But they can't compete with rock-hard humor. Comedy is the great lubricant, metaphorically, for easing people into tough discussions and, literally, for the few dudes who've wanted to bone me after seeing me do stand-up.

I wanna lube up the whole nation. And when I'm done lubing up the nation, I'm gonna take a giant tube of it to the world. I won't stop until we all just get along.

CHAPTER 1

Iranians Have No Gaydar and Other Things I Learned Growing Up in Palm Springs

I grew up in Palm Springs, California. Beyond its fame as the intellectual birthplace of one Negin Farsad, it's also internationally renowned as a golfing mecca and spa innovation center. You may know it as the leisure stronghold of the Rat Pack in the 1950s. Or perhaps you remember it fondly from that one episode of *Beverly Hills 90210* where everyone went to Palm Springs for President's Day Weekend.[1] And yet to others it's that "place where Sonny Bono was a mayor, or was that Carmel?" Needless to say, Palm Springs is a bird of many feathers.

---

1. There was a time in our nation's history where President's Day Weekend, not Spring Break, was the undisputed weekend for youthful debauchery, as commemorated by *Beverly Hills 90210*, a prestige drama from the '90s that many believe inspired *Breaking Bad*.

Palm Springs is not known for having a whole bunch of Middle Easterners. But the addition of me and my parents in the early '80s doubled that population to an unprecedented eight.[2] Though, technically, we're actually Iranian with a smattering of Azerbaijani. This smattering certainly doesn't mean anything to the average American, because the average American *doesn't know what Azerbaijan is*! (Please see Appendix A for clarification.) Let's just say I'm an ethnically brown Muz type who grew up in a resort town.

APPENDIX A

What Is This Azerbaijan Thing You Speak Of?
Is it a country, a type of banana, a Bulgarian MMA fighter, a manufacturer of thimbles? Totally unclear! Hint: If you guessed "a country that borders the north of Iran" then *ding ding ding*, you are correct! If you guessed that Iran has a province of the same name, you deserve accolades upon chocolate treats. And if you smell some kind of historical disputed territory situation, you get to read the rest of this book! There is a boatload of Azerbaijanis in Iran, they speak both Azeri (a dialect of Turkish) and Farsi (the language all those Iranians be speakin'). Iranians make jokes about Azeris in the way of "Polack" jokes or maybe "redneck" jokes, but funnier, much funnier. At the end of the day, there's a lot of love between the Farsi and Azeri speakers, a shared religion (Shia Islam), and my parents. And, by extension, me.

---

2. Me and my parents plus this one other family of 5: 3+5=8. "Show the proof," they say. And she did.

I was also the only kid on a solid, hardcore block of senior citizens. That block was then surrounded by an even larger neighborhood of…senior citizens. My childhood involved a lot of playing on the streets by myself, and then biking in those same streets, alone. And let's not forget those times I spent choreographing full-scale dance routines on the street while dodging oncoming Cadillacs— very slow-moving Cadillacs. Of course, those were solo dance routines. Because there were no other kids in my neighborhood. Because there were only senior citizens.

At some point in my childhood, my neighborhood started attracting gay gentlemen. You've probably heard this story before: Artists and gay peeps and gay artist peeps discover a downtrodden neighborhood, they start moving in, making it cool—suddenly mailboxes are adorned with a "design element" and gardening is replaced with "landscaping"—and their very cool presence drives up the prices, and suddenly there is more vegan cheese, and then the artists have to move out. They call it gentrification.

LIVING AMONG SENIOR CITIZENS, THE BULLET POINTS

☐ When you turn retirement age, you not only get a subscription to AARP but a zest for bedazzling sweatshirts.

☐ Senior citizens are afraid to open the door to little girls selling Girl Scout cookies, especially if they're accompanied by a mother who is only three inches taller than them.

☐ Old people tell really funny stories about the olden days,
so you should actually ask for those and make friends.
None of their stories involve the Internet.

☐ A lot of them are well versed in ballroom dancing.

☐ *Cocoon* was real.

☐ Cherry pie is too sweet, but a lemon loaf is just right.

The only difference is, in Palm Springs, the neigh-
borhoods weren't downtrodden. They were just full of
old people who didn't necessarily have the refined taste
to match a vintage weather vane with their midcentury
modern home. My immigrant parents bought one of
these houses that were designed by Frank Lloyd Wright
or Mies Van der Bloob or whoever. But they definitely
had no idea it was cool and were basically embarrassed
by how angular everything was. You know what all the
xenophobes say, "Those darned immigrants come to this
country and take all of our midcentury modern homes."
Guilty as charged.

But you know who knows how to appreciate the shit
out of a midcentury mod? Gay dudes! So they started
being our neighbors. I'm not saying they weren't old.
Most of them were still old. But they were gay, which
added a certain je ne sais quoi. Our neighborhood went
from "very sleepy" to "moderately sleepy" overnight.

In the Farsad home we had two rules: (1) never leave
your cup too close to the edge of a table; and (2) mis-
identify all gay neighbors as "roommates." Look, accord-

ing to former Iranian president Mahmoud Ahmadinejad, there are no gay people in Iran (please see Exhibit B). So my parents' gaydar wasn't just poorly functioning, it hadn't even been hooked up.

EXHIBIT B

Ridiculous Statements by Former President of Iran Mahmoud Ahmadinejad:
"In Iran, we don't have homosexuals, like in your country. We don't have that in our country. In Iran, we do not have this phenomenon. I don't know who's told you that we have it."

Hal and Bob were our neighbors. Hal was about six foot four and Bob was five foot two—Hal was black and Bob was white. So not only were these gentlemen rocking the boat by being a nonnormative[3] gay couple, they were also an interracial nonnormative gay couple and also an inter-height-al nonnormative gay couple! (Again, Bob was really short.) My parents loved them. They thought Hal and Bob were lovely, delightful, neighborly, and clearly *just roommates.*

The benefits of calling them roommates were manifold: (1) You didn't have to explain to your daughter what homosexuality was. (2) You didn't have to activate any homophobia, because deep down inside you're not even homophobic. (3) The word *roommates* has no larger sociopolitical implications. Roommates can be as interracial as they want!

---

3. Grad-school speak.

Roommates can be whatever gender they want! There is social pressure to hate the gays, but there is no such pressure to hate roommates.

Record Scratch!
Middle-of-the-Chapter Chapter Break to
Make a Technical Clarification on My Previous
Whereabouts

I feel like it's a bit misleading to start talking about my life in these pages in Palm Springs, California, when in fact, I actually started out my life in New Haven, Connecticut. I was there for my first two years of life and have no memories of it. Except to say that it must have worked on my subconscious, because later in life I applied to Yale...and was rejected. So, fuck Yale... is what I would say if I was still bitter about it, but I'm not bitter, right? So who cares. I hope Yale is happy and healthy and has a thousand little Yale babies and really rock-hard abs. I'm totally over it.

After those first two years, my parents moved me and my brother to Roanoke, Virginia. Roanoke wasn't in the glamorous "This is where *Homeland* was filmed" region of Virginia. Oh no. It's that part of Virginia that is "the South." In fact, when we left, and I started school in Palm Springs as a second grader, I was officially deemed the new girl at school, named Negin, who was Iranian but spoke with a redneck Southern accent. I would say things like "Y'all wanna play tetherball?" Now, a Southern accent on the West Coast already feels misplaced but coming out of the mouth of an ethnic second grader, that shit is bizarre.

Here's what I remember from Virginia: I had a best friend in preschool named Angela. Everyone in my class was blond. *Everyone.* The teachers thought I had a language problem, because I was pretty quiet and my parents spoke Farsi to me at home. They asked my parents to stop doing that.

My parents thought it was important for me to speak both Farsi and Azeri at home. Besides, my grandparents and most of my aunts and uncles didn't speak English, so speaking these other languages would be my only connection to them. Plus it's more fun to yell at little kids in Farsi. The first time I came home from a hard day of finger painting, snacking, and napping, I started speaking English to my parents. My dad panicked, and then he had a flash of brilliance: He pretended that he didn't understand English. That forced me to speak to him in Farsi. I took this on valiantly, considering myself some kind of three-year-old United Nations interpreter. From that point forth, I never ever spoke to them in English. To this day, it feels really weird to speak to them in English.

What my dumb little baby brain doesn't remember is that this was around the time of the Iran Hostage Crisis, which was a "total hoot" (I'm paraphrasing Ronald Reagan here). Here's the rundown if you don't know: Just after the Iranian Revolution, the new regime went nuts and took some hostages from the American embassy and held them for what seemed like *forever* (444 days). The American public was superpissed, which was sensible, because what the fuck? But the by-product of that super-pissed-ousity (new word) was anti-Iranian sentiment.

REAGAN WAS WEIRD ABOUT IRAN A LOT

First there's a hostage crisis in which we, the American people, learn that we're supposed to hate Iran. Got it. But then, Reagan decides to sell arms to Iran, then use the profits to fund the Sandinistas in Nicaragua. He had a thing for the Sandinistas and Congress was like "nuh-uh." So Reagan decided to creatively circumvent the law and fund them anyway. What's weirder was that at the time, we were also funding Iraq, which was in a war with Iran. What I'm saying is, we were supporting both sides in this war. It's like thumb-wrestling with yourself. This whole sordid affair became known as "The Iran-Contra Affair: A Nation Thumb-Wrestles with Itself." A guy named Oliver North took the fall, but various reports indicate that Reagan and George Bush the elder knew about it. But it didn't matter because the scandal slid off of all of them like a polyester romper. Bush went on to be president, and North went on to be a Fox News commentator.

When I was still being burped, my brother was already rolling through high school in that nonglamorous part of Virginia. Those days were tough because he was a mustachioed fourteen-year-old who had moved from Connecticut. So at first, the kids taunted him by calling him a Yank. The fact that *Yank* was still in use then was both

(a) deeply hilarious and (b) a wee little sign of the continued fissures in American society that have remained and festered so long after the Civil War.

Once the kids realized he wasn't a Yank but an *Iranian*, the bullying really ramped up. Feelings were hurt and punches were thrown. In many ways, because of the big age difference, my brother had to have the experience that I was protected from. He came to the United States not speaking English; he had to experience the most racist welcome; he grew facial hair far too early; and my mom dressed him like a middle-aged accountant. I'm not sure what would have happened to me if we had stayed in Virginia.

Reverse Record Scratch!
Back to Retirement Community High Jinks!

In Palm Springs I was a quiet kid. I didn't ruffle any feathers, I wasn't speaking up for justice, I wasn't fighting for causes. But all of that changed when I turned eight years old.

Imagine little Negin, wearing some really fly red corduroy pants (that looked more like high-waters because I kept growing out of them, but I refused to wear anything else). I was standing in line at the tetherball court, dutifully waiting my turn when Shelly Camonellie[4] cut in front of me. Yeah, she fucking *cut in front of me*. Now listen, I never had real athletic abilities. I couldn't bat a ball or volley a serve or racket a tennis. I was more your scholarly, thinking kid. *But* I fucking knew how to take

---

4. Come on, that's not her real name. What do I wanna do, get sued?

people down on the tetherball court. I was quite good. I could serve a ball with sheer force (no bosom getting in my way). The ball would whip around and around and around that pole. The sun would glisten off my knuckles. I could suddenly speak Portuguese and my feet would slightly levitate off the ground. I left other kids in the dust, crying and urinating all over themselves.[5]

TETHERBALL: FROM "VIOLENT" TO "PLAYGROUND"

The history of tetherball has long been disputed. Or rather it hasn't been disputed so much as nobody really cares. But, the earliest account of tetherball goes back to ninth-century Tatars who lived in modern day Russia, Ukraine, Uzbekistan, and Kazakhstan. As the story goes, Tatars would take the head of a vanquished enemy, attach it with a rope to a pole, and then beat it with a stick. Now, it's a really fun playground activity for children.

But Shelly Camonellie…oh Shelly! She didn't want to see me have a good life. She wanted to take over the court and bully the rest of us into submission. She was good at that. But on this day, of my eighth year, nestled in the badass resort town of Palm Springs, where manicured golf courses bring grown men to their knees, I, Negin Farsad, told her off. I said to Shelly, "Suck my dick, Shelly

---

5. That explains the old adage, "You've never seen good tetherball till you've urinated yourself."

Camonellie." Now, I was eight years old, so I didn't know what a dick was or what sucking had to do with it. But I had heard the phrase before from some fifth graders and I knew, intuitively, that it applied to this situation.

I was a perfect student with perfect grades and perfect attendance. I'm talking straight A's. I never got in trouble. But on this, the "Suck my dick, Shelly Camonellie" day, a teacher overheard me. I was immediately scolded, embarrassed in front of a jury of tetherballians, and taken to the principal's office, where I was sentenced to Lunch on the Stage.

The cafeteria was totally regular looking and also doubled as a theatre for elementary school productions. But during lunchtime, that cafeteria stage had a very sinister use. Very "bad" students were punished by having to eat lunch in silence on that stage, facing all the "good" students.

This was my first brush with public performance. At first, it was humiliating. But a few minutes in, I realized that my reputation was altering. I wasn't simply the goody-two-shoes girl that never got in trouble. I was the girl who stood up for myself and told people to "suck a D"—whatever that was. I could eat tater tots in front of dozens of kids and not break. And in a most ridiculous fashion this act of civil disobedience—*yes, Thoreau!*—made me realize that I can stand up for things. That standing up for things wouldn't kill me.

A year later I stood up for myself on something that wasn't about tetherball dominance. The elementary school didn't want to put me in the gifted and talented program in fourth grade. I think it had something to do with my abilities in English. I knew instinctively that being in this gifted and talented program was going to have major life consequences. We put kids on tracks in this country, and that determines everything about where that kid will end up all the way through college and beyond.

So, I put my emboldened pants on, the way only nine-year-olds (and North Korean despots) do, and marched into the principal's office. I recruited my mother for support. In her thickly accented English, she said, "Vhy isn't my daughter in ze class for ze smart children?" They hemmed and hawed, and we got our way.

Yeah! Civil Disobedience, motherfuckers! Ain't nobody gonna not put me in the non–gifted and talented classes… wait, huh? I mean, Ain't nobody gonna keep me outta the classes that aren't… *Oh*, double negatives, you got me again!

Showing up for the fight became something I did over and over again in life. But as is my custom, I tried to make the fight funny. As the old saying goes, you attract softer punches when you're wearing a clown nose.

I grew up and kept fighting. But, my adult kerfuffles have a lot less to do with tetherball. Here's one of my more recent fights:

The New York City MTA Up and Ran Some Bigoted Ads

In the fall of 2014, the MTA put up posters all over the subway and bus system that promoted hatred of Muslims. A known hate group, headed by a very loud and public

Muslim basher, raised $100,000 for the campaign. That money could go very far, because the MTA subway system sees over five million eyeballs a day, or rather ten million eyeballs and five million pairs of eyeballs, assuming all the eyeballs come in pairs. My point is, that's a lot of people consuming gleefully hate-filled messages urging them that Muslims suck.[6]

This wasn't even the first time that this Unpleasant Bigot spent that kind of money to put up posters. She also spent money to make the Ground Zero Mosque a controversy—the thing that wasn't even a mosque but an Islamic cultural center. She had all of America talking about the Ground Zero Mosque, as if a few blocks away from Ground Zero was sacred, as if that one strip of land sandwiched between a Subway (pun intended) and a strip club was in any way hallowed ground. But she's got some other impressive credits to her name; for example, she's on the Southern Poverty Law Center's very elite, very hard-to-get-on list of hate groups. She was also praised for her work by a neo-Nazi gentleman who goes by the moniker "skinjob88"—he's apparently *very* hard to impress.

With the hundreds of thousands that this Unpleasant Bigot spends on the Muz-hate machine, she could have bought a property in Belize with multiple custom-made rocking chairs. She could have bought her own binder clip company. She could have spent it all on an entire city's

---

6. Maybe you've noticed that I didn't name the group, the ringleader, or the actual content of the posters. I really don't want to add to their publicity machine, but if you're interested, as Sergey Brin once said, "Bing it."

lifetime supply of bubble gum. Well, maybe a small city like Boca Raton, FL. She could have done anything, anything else, instead of spend the money on hate.

To add further insult to injury, the Unpleasant Bigot's posters were exceptionally unattractive and poorly designed. They were all negative space, ridiculous lettering, and low-resolution images. If you're going to be bigoted, at least choose a better font.

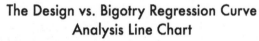

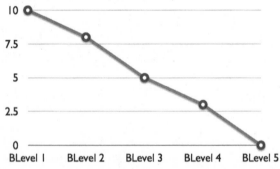

This curve illustrates that as bigotry increases, design sensitivity decreases. Basically, the more bigoted you are, the more likely you are to make something ugly.

The MTA was trying to get out of posting them but a court order, citing free speech, forced them into it. I, for one, can't get enough of that First Amendment. Sure, it protects hate speech, but that's what "freedom of speech" has to mean. It can't play favorites, it can't create a clique of "cool speech" and "super unpopular speech," like it's a mean girl in high school. Freedom of speech has to accept everything. Parents can't have a favorite child, and freedom of speech can't distinguish between hate speech and...er...great speech.

FREE SPEECH IN OTHER COUNTRIES

Our free speech rights are totally dope! The bee's knees! The mom's jugs! All'a that. But it's easy to take it for granted. You could hop over to some European countries and you'll definitely get better coffee and non-GMO foods, but you will not know where you stand on freedom of speech. Some of their rules are fuzzy; they ban some forms of speech but not others. In France, everyone has "freedom of speech," but there it means you cannot deny the Jewish Holocaust but you *can* deny the Armenian Genocide. Weird right? After the *Charlie Hebdo* attacks, sixty-nine people were arrested in France for defending terrorism. Jail!* Some of those were teenagers sending around ironic cartoons. Hate speech or speech that is suspected of inciting racial hatred does not get protected in fancy countries like the UK, Belgium, the Netherlands, Germany, and Denmark. So basically, if you ever want to do any "opinion expressing," America is the least confusing place to do it. The rest of the world has really complicated speech laws that probably have hidden riders like the number of bowls of red M&M's that are supposed to be in the green room. It's a mess.

*See Ali Abunimah, "France Begins Jailing People for Ironic Comments," *Electronic Intifada*, https://electronicintifada.net/blogs/ali-abunimah /france-begins-jailing-people-ironic-comments; and "The Sound of Silence," *Economist*, http://www.economist.com/news/international /21640324-reactions-paris-attacks-highlight-threats-free-expression -around-world.

So while I was disappointed that the posters had to go up, I was also glad that we live in a system where the posters *could* go up. In New York, some individuals and groups took it upon themselves to deface the hate-filled posters. I understand that because it's hard to look at them when they're talking about you, or a neighbor you love, or an aunt by marriage that makes great muffins. But to me, defacing wasn't going to be helpful. Defacing shuts down the conversation.

My options for retaliation were: (a) stand in front of each poster yelling at passersby, "Don't look at this poster!" (b) shutter myself at home for a month and order Pad Thai until the posters were gone; or (c) make my own posters.

So I called up my fellow Muslim comedy buddy Dean Obeidallah[7] and I said, "How about we raise the money to put up a series of delightful posters about Muslims? And, is it possible to get a zit on your toe? Because I think I have a zit on my toe."* After five solid minutes of research we figured out that the minimum ad buy for the MTA was in the neighborhood of $17,000. We didn't think we could raise as much money as that other group did, but $17,000–$20,000 was within our begging capacity.

We went online, shared a PayPal button, and within three days we had raised about $19,156.24 or thereabouts. And with it, we designed a couple dozen posters, put them online for feedback and narrowed it down to these lucky six.

---

7. Dean is of the Palestinian-American-Italian variety, he's wonderful, a stand-up guy and a stand-up comedian, and he enjoys standing.
*The posters also promote our film *The Muslims Are Coming!* but I'll talk about that more later.

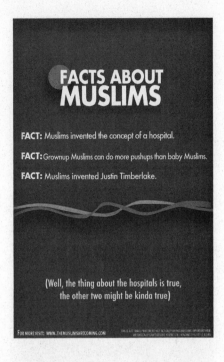

MUSLIMS!
They invented coffee, the toothbrush, and algebra...
Oh wait, sorry about the algebra.
That's a year of class you'll never get back.
FOR MORE VISIT: WWW.THEMUSLIMSARECOMING.COM

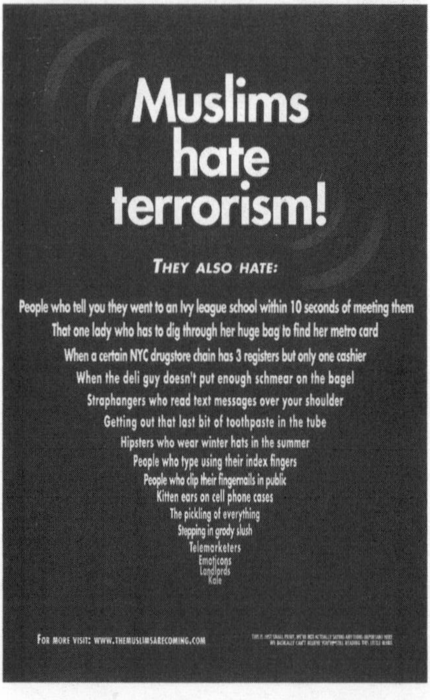
Muslims hate terrorism!
THEY ALSO HATE:
People who tell you they went to an Ivy league school within 10 seconds of meeting them
That one lady who has to dig through her huge bag to find her metro card
When a certain NYC drugstore chain has 3 registers but only one cashier
When the deli guy doesn't put enough schmear on the bagel
Straphangers who read text messages over your shoulder
Getting out that last bit of toothpaste in the tube
Hipsters who wear winter hats in the summer
People who type using their index fingers
People who clip their fingernails in public
Kitten ears on cell phone cases
The pickling of everything
Stepping in grody slush
Telemarketers
Emoticons
Landlords
Kale
FOR MORE VISIT: WWW.THEMUSLIMSARECOMING.COM

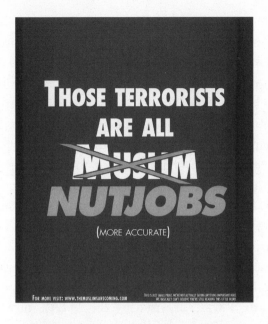

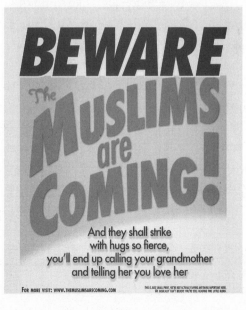

The Fighting Bigotry with Delightful Posters Campaign was an interesting challenge because we had to work with the MTA, a pseudo-public-private entity. It serves a huge ridership and does great work in that arena, but it is also a slow-moving bureaucracy that can drive you so crazy you end up scrubbing the grout in your bathroom. Some aspects of these posters didn't make the final cut. For example, we weren't allowed to make the joke in very small font on the very bottom right of the poster that said, "Defamers, draw penis here." For those of you who don't live in New York, it was a nod to the fact that subway posters always get penises drawn on them.[8]

We weren't allowed to use the words *poo* or *genitals*, and we even had to change our font at one point. At every turn, I was surprised by the MTA's nitpicks; the word *poo* used comedically was bad, but like an entire poster campaign preaching hate of Muslims was totally fine. *What???* But we worked with them every step of the way and tried to remain delightful, because you will attract more bees with honey. After five months we had a date—on April 28, 2015, our posters were set to go.

Then there was a hiccup: The MTA decided to ban all political content. They made that rule change on April 29, 2015, the day after our posters were supposed to go up. But through an innovation of time travel, the law was imposed a day before it actually took effect.[9] What's

8. Oh, yes, I'm seeing it now: penises have come up twice in the same chapter and both in a drawing context. I don't know what that says about me, but talk among yourselves.
9. Yes, the New York City MTA has the ability to time-travel.

crazy is that somehow, Muslims and their frittata recipes are considered "political" content. We've somehow gotten to the point where just saying the word *Muslim* makes something political. It isn't. And in our case, it's a joke.

Afterward, we got tired and decided to shut up about it. *Kidding!* We decided to get legal. We launched the Fighting bigotry with a Delightful Lawsuit campaign. Our First Amendment rights got sucker-punched, and we wanted to punch back. Besides, if you let someone like the Unpleasant Bigot do awful anti-Muslim poster campaigns, you have to let the comedians do one fun and loving campaign, right? You have to let Muslims tell the story they want to tell, right? If you're gonna let Victoria's Secret show hot ladies peddling lingerie, you gotta let everyone sell the thing they're trying to sell. And what I'm trying to sell is that Muslims are hilarious.[10]

A few months later, the court rendered a decision, siding with...THE COMEDIANS. That's right, a couple of lowlife comics took on the MTA and the comics won. Judge Colleen McMahon reminded the MTA that the posters aren't political "unless we have reached the unhappy moment in this country where the mere mention of one of the three Abrahamic faiths is 'prominently or predominantly political' simply because that faith is Islam." We *haven't* reached that unhappy moment so the MTA has to put them up because LAW told them so. I had never quite experienced this particular feeling of

---

10. And, of course, we also promoted the film *The Muslims Are Coming!*, featured on every poster.

victory. I imagined it was what hot blond girls feel like
every day.[11]

The MTA got this one wrong, but the F train still got
me to my gigs on time, so at least it was doing its pri-
mary job. Tetherball was where the fight began. And the
fight has taken me to some interesting places since then.
So thank you Shelly Camonellie for trying *and failing* to
ruin my life.

---

11. Those posters finally went up in the NYC subway system and I had
the very good fortune of actually seeing people look at a poster and
chuckle. One chuckle won't change social systems but add enough chuck-
les up—like millions of them—and that could amount to real change.

CHAPTER 2

Hairy Legs, Short Shorts, and the Mexification of Negin Farsad

I mentioned I grew up feeling black. Except that in Palm Springs, the only black people we had were Mexican. So I initially went with that.

Palm Springs High School was over 40 percent Mexican.[1] As a student there, I was one of two Iranian-Americans in my class. The other Iranian was the kind of kid you could picture having a pet iguana (and in fact, he *had* a pet iguana), so our friendship was a nonstarter. People expected us to be friends because we were both Iranians, but I have a strict No Pet Reptiles friendship policy. I'm sure you understand.

---

1. This is a total anecdotal statistic, I don't have real records to prove it. But my eyeballs were record enough for me back then.

No Reptiles Allowed in This Friendship

I also didn't have Mexican friends because…well, I was strange. But I envied them. They had groups and cliques—an Identity! They had their own slang and dress code and *Sabado Gigante*!

And there it is, the crux of being an Iranian-American Muslim in Palm Springs, or a Romanian-American Greek Orthodox or a Sri Lankan–American Buddhist or a Belgo-Bulgarian-neo-Pagan Cotton Candy adherent: *You have no posse!* No large-scale peer group. You're just sorta riding the cultural train solo, which is totally sad. So if you're like me, you glom onto other, more populated minority groups. Sometimes they accept you, sometimes you join the drama club.

I could best be classified as "that one ethnic girl on campus who dressed like the love child of Kurt Cobain and a drunk Roma gypsy." I was all Doc Martins and burgundy lipstick, large T-shirts and colorful Iranian scarves. It was a look, to say the least.

Yet I still viewed the Mexican plight as my own. I saw the debate over immigration grow and grow and turn as ugly and resistant as a calcified bunion on the big toe of

America. And for its part, Palm Springs was an extreme example of what was happening in the country:

There were the Old Rich People—they were the ones with all the money and the extreme landscaping needs. There were the Leisurely People, some gay, all somehow independently wealthy—these were the people who weren't that old and kept a winter house in Palm Springs, and could afford to jet around and make the desert one of their many stomping grounds. These people had hard-ons for cacti and air-conditioning.

Then there were the People Who Had Regular Jobs, which consisted of a slew of minorities and a handful of middle-class white folk. Overwhelmingly, the People with Jobs were Mexicans; underwhelmingly, they were my parents.

**Palm Springs Population as understood by Negin Farsad:
A Highly Scientific Pie Chart Based on a Sample Set of One***

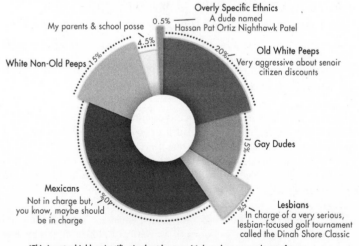

*This is not a highly scientific pie chart because it's based on a sample set of one

The Mexicans took the jobs nobody else wanted, did hard honest work, and at the end of the day came home to insulting news reports about how they were stealing jobs or how we should be an English-only country or about how Del Taco was considered Mexican cuisine. Despite their vast numbers at my school, they self-segregated, had their own popular people and did their own thing. But did they actually self-segregate? Or, like the nerds, did they not feel welcome in mainstream white culture? I didn't feel too welcome. I got straight A's and could grow a beard better than any of the boys in my class. Plus I was a member of one of those stupidly underpopulated ethnic minorities.

So I longed to hang out with the Mexican kids, to throw down Spanish slang, to celebrate my fifteenth birthday like it was a really big deal.[2] On the surface, I looked like an Iranian-American-Punk-Gypsy-Goth girl. On the inside, I said things like "We gotta take the mantle of Cesar Chavez and fight for worker's rights, man." And I said it in the voice of the Taco Bell Chihuahua. This may sound culturally insensitive to you. But there was no such thing as cultural sensitivity when I was growing up...eh...it was a lot like today.

---

2. Vagina-bearing Mexican-Americans celebrate their fifteenth birthdays like it's a really big deal. It's called a quinceañera, and it looks really fun and horribly awkward at the same time, sort of like a Bar Mitzvah.*
* Penis-bearing Jewish-Americans celebrate their thirteenth birthdays like it's a really big deal. It's called a Bar Mitzvah and it looks really fun and horribly awkward, sort of like a quinceañera.^
^ Vagina-bearing Jewish-Americans celebrate something like Bar Mitvahs and quinceañeras called Bat Mitzvahs, which are similarly fun and awkward but with more mentions of a mystical Bubby and zombie-like slow dancing.

The Taco Bell Chihuahua was taken off commercials in 2000. But take heart, ridiculous cultural icons still abound! To this day, the Washington Redskins are still called *the Washington Redskins*. The term *redskin* has a very negative history, not unlike the N-word for the black community. Luckily we have gotten to the point where horrible images of black Americans as coons, sambos, brutes, etc., are less and less common and are deemed socially unacceptable. The Washington Redskins would never be called The Washington N-words—that would be shockingly outrageous!! There is cultural policing on that score. But Native Americans are one of those underpopulated groups—you know, because American settlers were really effective at killing them. (It's one of those early American ideals that we don't talk about when we're rubbing one out to our Founding Fathers.) We have a blind spot for some groups when it comes this kind of icon building.

Where being a Mexican really had an advantage was roll call. All the teachers were familiar with the iconic American names—the multiple Jennifers and Chads had nothing to be embarrassed about (even though you'd think being just another "Chad" would be embarrassing—it wasn't; it made you more acceptable). But my teachers in Palm Springs were also familiar with all the iconic Mexican names. The Rodrigos and Juans, the Aurelias and Marianas. But there was no such familiarity with the ol' Iranian names.

I had a teacher my sophomore year who would run down the attendance sheet and roll her *r*'s real good

for Veronica and Gabriela, she would get her May-
flower twang on for Greg and Jennifer and then it got to
me: "Megan?" No, Negin.[3] "Megeen?" No, Neh-geen.
"Megreen?" No…and then she busted out with *Noodle*?
That's right, she called me *Noodle Farsad*. And then she
laughed, laughed *hard* at her own joke.[4]

She ultimately settled on calling me NF. For the entire
semester. Because she admitted that she just couldn't get
it right, "and it will be easier if I just call you NF."

---

3. By the way, the proper pronunciation is "Neh-geen"—hard *g* like in
"begin," and the end rhymes with "magazine."
4. "Noodle" doesn't even make sense for an Iranian-American. Rice
Farsad or better yet, Saffron Farsad would have been more accurate, but
my name starts with an *N* so…I understand her struggle.

I don't know if your high school was like this, but our Sex Ed and Drivers Ed were the same class. So the teacher would spend the first half of class talking about three-point turnabouts, then switch her focus to what happens in the backseats of cars: hardcore fucking. I could handle being "NF'd" during the car talk, "NF, are you supposed to yield to left-turning cars in a two-lane street?" But Sex Ed was harder to, um, swallow. "What is the function of the labia, NF?"

There I was, Noodle Farsad. My dreams of rubbing elbows with Mexican cool kids were quickly fading. I could recruit only one solid Mexican into my fold. His name was Leonard. He would later change that to Leonardo because of the obvious "Le-Nerd" iteration of his name. (He also later came out of the closet as a gay Mexican, which is a crossover category, so he got ten points for that.) Le-nerd would tell me amazing stories about his culture; one of them was about the Thanksgiving Bean. You know how regular American families like to have a stuffed turkey for holidays? Well, in Mexican families, they like to have a giant stuffed bean. Basically, they take a bean and grow it all year long till it's as large as a turkey. And then, for holiday dinners, they stuff that bean with rice and salsa and smaller beans.

How fascinating! What an interesting tidbit about Mexican culture! I went around telling every old, gay neighbor I could find about this beautiful Mexican tradition. The beans that bring them together for our nation's most treasured holidays. What a thoughtful way to fuse American and Mexican cultural heritage, I thought. I could just picture vast Mexican landscapes covered with plump beans. Cheerful visitors going on their annual giant bean-picking trip—which is a lot like pumpkin picking but it's bean picking. I pictured Mexican families walking along bean patches, a smiling papito laughing at how big the bean is and pretending it's too heavy to carry. A little niñita satisfied that her parents picked the bean that she, not her little brother, wanted. The mamita thinking she should pick up a family sized bottle of Beano for their holiday dinner, because we all know how Abuelo gets! My mind went places. I told people, so many people, about this interesting facet of Mexican culture. Until I found out that Leonard was lying. Like a Mexican.*

Despite my best efforts, by senior year, I had only two Mexicans in my address book.[5] They were solid, and one of them was even a bestie, but I was far from embraced by the larger (cooler) Mexican population on campus. I couldn't figure it out, and the sheer exhaustion led me to a high-profile position as Academic Nerd and Drama Geek Crossover girl. It took a truly special person from the league of dorkdom to have been both the president of the debate society *and* vice president of the drama club. Having excelled in calculus *and* to have painted theatrical sets after school, I was that kind of truly special dork.

My best friend, Anca, was a volleyball-playing Romanian immigrant who had no other Romanians to lean on. We shared a deep and abiding embarrassment over our

---

*This is a joke.
5. That was a hard-copy set of little papers where we wrote down people's phone numbers. This was before cell phones.

immigrant parents. If you got a good grade they never said, "Hey, great job." In both our mother countries, good grades were assumed, not celebrated. As girls, boys were forbidden or at best tolerated. For us, high school was a series of lies: "I'm going to drama practice." (Read: I'm going to the Homecoming Dance that I'm not allowed to go to.) Or if my mother asked me why I was wearing pants when it was so hot out, I would say, "Oh, my body temperature is so weird, it doesn't even feel like ninety degrees." (Read: I wasn't allowed to shave my legs until I was sixteen! *Sixteen!* So my hairy-legged humiliation in high school—located in the *desert* of *Southern California*—was constant.)

We also never knew quite where we fit in. Throughout high school, among the college-obsessed nerdbombs, there was a constant debate over affirmative action. People endlessly questioned whether it was fair for black and Mexican students to have a leg up, or could it really be defined as a leg up if there was never a level playing field to begin with—we asked all the typical questions on the issue. It was heated and emotional for a lot of students who felt that they were being slighted by the system. It was an interesting discussion, but I always wondered how colleges saw *me* in this debate. I didn't think I deserved a leg up, but at the same time I didn't want to be treated as any Tom, Dick, and Harry who submitted an application. The debate over college admissions seemed to fortify the binary discussion of race, and it continued to leave me and my hyphenated peeps in the lurch. For example, if anyone looked at Anca, they would think she was white.

But she was born in communist Romania. Her life there didn't involve any white privilege. Her immigrant struggle involved...struggle...so would college admissions think of her as white? All we could hope to do was mark the X in the box next to "Other."

The lure of Mexicans for me, as an unclassifiable minority, was still strong—they were still the biggest legitimately recognized hyphenated-American group in town—and it came to a head senior year of high school when Essy—the one other Iranian kid in my grade, who at this point had dissociated himself from his reptile friends—started dating a Mexican girl from the ESL program.

Our high school had a sizable English as a Second Language program, and Essy managed to charm one of the girls in this group. Did they speak one another's language? Not quite. Did they speak the language of lust? *Definitely.*

A romantic pairing like this rarely happened. The sectarian fissures in our school ran deep. As any '90s movie about high school will tell you, the jocks stuck with the cheerleaders, the grade-obsessed competitively leeched off each other's homework, and the theatre people melodramatically walked the halls in turtlenecks. But here was this Iranian-American Muslim kid, who took only Advanced Placement classes, going after a Mexican immigrant in ESL. It just wasn't done. The student body looked at them like they had jungle fever. It was like *Guess Who's Coming to Dinner*, except dinner involved tortillas and no shared language and it was actually a lunch high in trans fats served in the poorly lit school cafeteria.

Essy was rejecting the high school classifications passed down by generations of pent-up hierarchy fanatics. Sure, he mostly wanted to get to second base with a chick, but on a subconscious level, Essy was seeking a cross-cultural coalition.

And actually, a Mexican girlfriend made perfect sense for an Iranian dude. Both parties were immigrants' kids with strict parents. Both parties had a more flavorful handle on food. Both got their grandmothers to dance at parties. And both had sun-tolerant skin. It was a marriage born in an American melting pot! (Or American salad bowl or mosaic or scrapbook or vase of potpourri or any other things-mixed-into-a-thing metaphor.)

But the haters looked at both sets of immigrants as objects of concern. And it helped *them* for *us* to be divided. I've performed all over the country and one thing has always been true: you rarely ever meet someone who *loves the Muslims*! But *hates the Mexicans*! You never hear someone say "Asians are the worst! But African-Americans are the best!" If you hate one group, you're kind of likely to hate them all. So often my question is: Why aren't minorities in the United States building bridges and finding that commonality?

At the end of the day, minorities of every stripe are all actually in the same boat. And that boat is full of compost. Because in the 1990s the Taco Bell Chihuahua was dressed in a beret to look like Che Guevara—not unlike today's depiction of the hook-nosed Muslim terrorist, which itself is derived from the old stereotype of the miserly Jew. The Washington Redskins mascot matters to all of us—turn it one degree the other way and it's The Washington Terrorists, or the Washington Sambos, or The Washington Brownskin Terrorist Sambo Bagels. What was it about "the silence of our friends"?[6]

Minority groups should form strategic alliances, because the bigotry one group faces is just another side of the bigotry another group faces. Bigotry is very predictable that way.

What was striking about Essy and his Mexican girlfriend was that we all found it so...striking. But why would we? Their experiences in the world as hyphenated-Americans are so very similar. Minorities should come together, because they understand what its like to be a minority in the United States. The only difference is that some of us are a part of the popular cultural discourse, and some of us aren't. Luckily those differences didn't stop those darned kids from making out behind the bleachers during first period.

6. It's from a Martin Luther King Jr. quote: "In the end, we will remember not the words of our enemies, but the silence of our friends."

CHAPTER 3

Negin and the Terrible, Horrible, No Good, Very Bad Day

aka High School

Everyone has that quintessentially awful and horribly beleaguered high school moment. It's that instance where all the good that high school provides—academic preparation for college, young adult socialization, Funyons—is sucked into oblivion and replaced by something terribly embarrassing.

I did an interview with comedian Brian Posehn for my film *Nerdcore Rising*. (Oh yeah, later in life I would make a feature documentary about nerds who rap called *Nerdcore Rising*. It's very nerdy, as in Weird Al Yankovic is in it, that's how nerdy it is. Though to be clear, Weird Al is a gentleman among mere nerdleman and should run for president of the United States, but I would totally support him if he wanted to run for president of a smaller, less demanding country, or student body president of a high school that would bend the rules and let him run.) But anyway, back to Brian Posehn,[1] the inimitable nerdian-American who, by this point, had a stellar career in stand-up comedy and an equally stellar career in comic books and also played a damned fine gay neighbor in the *Sarah Silverman Program*.

Brian told a story about his first day of high school. He arrived on campus with his best friends from middle school, excited about what the year would hold. But on that first morning his best friends decided to diss him—they calculated that Brian, who dressed like a geek and had weird interests, would drag them down. Some might call this an "efficient cost-benefit analysis" others might call it "dickholery." That was the last time his friends ever acknowledged him. He cried as he told this story—a man who at this point was in his thirties and had legitimately succeeded in Hollywood—he full-on cried. I bet you that memory taints everything that happened for him in high school, like pit stains that will never wash out of your favorite T-shirt from that one band you claim you discovered.

For me, it was this: I was a drama geek and as such it was my duty to *be in plays*. I took this very seriously. Our

---

1. You're probably wondering what my position is on Brian Posehn's presidential standing, since I went in depth on Weird Al's. Well, while I think Posehn is an astute scholar and human, his skills are better suited to a VP role. Basically, a joint ticket with Weird Al and Brian Posehn could do wonders for our country, or any smaller country.

entire department took this very seriously. We all thought we were little Dame Judi Denches, running around being professional actors. There were auditions, cast lists were posted, cheers of exhalation were walloped, tears were shed. It was such an emotional thing, you didn't know if you were walking into a Jazzercise championship, an obstetrics delivery room, or a high school theatre class. Like our rivals, the sports people, we dedicated our lives to it. We rehearsed every day after school, we built sets on weekends, we memorized lines between periods. So when I was cast in something it was serious business.

Each semester the drama department was called upon to share (promote) what we were doing at Assembly. Assembly is that frightful collection in one room of all the students in the school. A brew of teenaged angst, optimism, hormonal depravity, SweeTarts, backpacks with one of the pocket zippers open, and shame. It was held over a few periods, because we had a big school and not everyone could fit into our small theatre at the same time.

We presented the funniest scenes from this play for Assembly repeatedly over three or four periods. It was the last show of the day, and the moment came where the main dude character has to choose between us gals. I was on stage left wearing a black dress, and the other girl was stage right wearing a red dress. The guy stood in the middle, comically hesitating and fumbling through a soliloquy about whom he should choose. He made the case for choosing me, at which point one kid in the audience yelled out, "Don't choose that fat ugly bitch." He yelled this in front of three hundred people. The fat ugly bitch he was referring to was me.

Then dozens more voices joined the chorus—"Yeah, that bitch is fat," "Fuck that ugly bitch," "Yo homey, she fugly," etc., etc. I'm paraphrasing, here because I couldn't make out every single one of the many ways in which they told me I was a hideous monster.

At that point the main dude (and my buddy Steven) had to make the case for the girl in the red dress, and the audience cheered—"Yeah, choose her, choose the red dress!" "She's hot, don't go for the ugly bitch," "Yeah, go get that blondy," etc. Again, I'm paraphrasing because they all chose the blond girl with their own special locution. Little did they know that we had created an entire backstory for the blond character in which she's really into taxidermy and eating dry ramen. But you know, those are the kinds of nuggets that the audience just isn't privy to. Alas, unfortunately for them, and their clear fetishization of red dresses, the playwright chooses the Iranian-American girl with black hair.

I can't quite tell you what it feels like to stand up in front of three hundred people and hear them call you fat and ugly. In high school, it amounts to *the worst day of your life*. Or as I called it then, "This is worse than the one day my mom caught me borrowing $20 from her purse." Or "This is worse than the one time Drew told everyone I liked him and I swear to God I didn't but like multiple people thought I did." Or better yet, "This is worse than getting rejected from Yale"—kidding, I'm totally over that rejection! I don't care about Yale any-more! That's a crazy comparison!

I do remember that feeling of insecurity as a sixteen-year-old girl—that feeling that I wasn't pretty like the blond girls. The fear that I would never amount to anything in the social world because I just didn't look like them. Never mind the fact that I had a creeping anxiety over developing bunions.[2] I wasn't given the right nose, the right skin, the right physique, the right ethnicity. I compared myself endlessly with white girls who seemed to control our school—despite the fact that the Latino population was huge, they *still* seemed to reign supreme. I mean, shit, they all looked like magazine cutouts. To hear three hundred people affirming every crappy, inse-cure thought I had in my head—in Surround Sound—was more than my little sixteen-year-old heart could handle.

I wanted the stage to swallow me as the minutes—which felt like anthropological eras—went by. I wanted to run home to my mother to be (a) consoled but also (b) to yell at her for not listening to me, I told her a mil-lion times that if she let me shop at Hot Topic. maybe I wouldn't be having such a rough day! At the time, I took the words of three hundred kids as objective truth. Like 4 out of 5 doctors agree that Sensodyne is the best toothpaste, 300 out of 300 high school kids agree that Noodle Farsad ain't worth shit. I went around believing that for a long time.

---

2. This turned out to be a false fear, as I have yet to develop bunions. My pinky toe, however, has never really pulled its weight, but that's a story for another time.

To be clear, it was more than my little sixteen-year-old heart could handle *internally*. Internally I was a mess. But externally I did my job. I was an actor, and fuck those little shitstains for trying to distract my laser-like focus from playing the part. The part of a funny girl onstage, that I was born to play. I was going for a Juliette Binoche meets Mike Myers, and lemme just say two words: Oscar worthy.

For some reason I didn't take note of the audience. If I had taken a closer look, I would have gone on my own rant: You, Dan McDickhole, in the front row! You have an uncontrolled erection that you got from a stapler. You, Man Boobs Johnson, you actually said "Mexicans speak Mexicano" in history class. You, Fart Machine Finley, you dipped nachos into your milk shake at lunch.

When the scene was over, me and the other girl had to go backstage for a costume change. I was shell-shocked and a tear slid down my face—you know that single tear you see in movies on the protagonist's face that makes you lose your shit? You know that one tear that an actor releases when the moment is just right and you wonder if there's a production assistant waiving an onion off screen? I had that stupid single tear. That one dumb little tear carried the weight of every crush I ever had that didn't like me back, all the times I regretted having an extra French fry, all the times I tried to make myself look cute with lip gloss. If that tear could talk!

The girl in the red dress saw the tear and was speechless, she tried to say something that would let me know that what just happened was not okay by her standards of polite teenaged society. I wanted to tell her, don't worry because according to John Hughes movies I win in the end and according to Scorsese movies, the audience ends up being strangled by a dude named "Fingers" in the backseat of a Lincoln Continental.

Mrs. Rosemary Mallett, our drama teacher, ran backstage and said, "This Assembly will be over soon." Basically, what she meant was, just go out there again, in front of a bunch of hungry shape-shifting wolves, and do your job. I wiped that one stupid tear, threw on the other costume and ran out to do my closing lines. "Never let them see you cry"—an old adage that was developed by seventh-century Huns[3] but repurposed by a sixteen-year-old girl in Palm Springs, California, centuries later. I took a bow. I appeared unrattled.

I ran out of the theatre when the bell rang, I went to the parking lot through the back of the school so no one would see me, hopped in my parents' old Honda Accord hatchback, and was the first one off campus. The car had an all-black vinyl interior, which in the heat of the desert meant "ass burns." I pretended like my buns felt normal and drove directly to the nearest Vons supermarket, where I bought a six-pack of orange Creamsicles.

I came home and couldn't speak, but my mom knew something was wrong. My best friend, Anca, came over. I didn't have to tell her what happened, because she'd heard about it in the hallways; it was the whisper of every

---

3. Yeah, I don't know who said that first—I can't find an attribution—so let's just say "seventh-century Huns of Central Asia." They never get credit for anything.

locker conversation (locker conversations are the widely regarded inspiration behind "Page Six," *People* magazine, and *Lockers Weekly*). We ate Creamsicles, cried a little, and mostly strategized on how to get the Sri Lankan girl and the Indian guy in our grade to go to prom together.[4]

The next day the teachers from the guilty classes asked Mrs. Mallet if they could formally apologize, but I just wanted to forget it. Mrs. Mallett handled it like a pro, she didn't dignify the hoots and hollers, and offered the drama room as a safe haven for me to skip calculus.

Mrs. Mallett made a comedian out of me that day because, well, come on—you wanna heckle me? Bring it! What was even more remarkable about her is that she cast me—*me*—as the hot girl in a play. She did stuff like that—she also cast me in the male part of God's messenger in Neil Simon's *God's Favorite*. She never saw hotness defined in a certain way or the representative of "God" defined in a certain way. For her, a Jewish Neil Simon wrote about a Christian dude who meets God's messenger, that was best played by an Iranian-American Muslim gal. That was normal to her. And it is! She didn't give a shit how you saw it, because she knew the vision of society she had in her head and that vision was right. And everyone else could suck it.

She taught me two essential lessons: (1) hecklers will never disappear, so you have to learn not to give a shit. There are YouTube comments piled upon mean tweets

---

4. PS: We totally succeeded in getting them to go to prom together! We were a fabulous posse of Iranian, Indian, Sri Lankan, Romanian, and some white guys at prom.

that will never let you forget that you have opposition. Irrational, ugly opposition. But you cannot give a *shit*. And (2) if you don't like reality, cast it differently. *Present* it differently. Who cares if God is normally an old white guy with a beard? That's just not how I see it. Who cares if beauty is often a blond woman in a red dress? That's just not how I see it. I'm casting beauty, and today it looks different.

I never spoke of this episode to a soul outside the school, not even my mother. Years later I managed to tell a friend as we were exchanging high school horror stories. But I haven't figured out how to frame it as a funny and embarrassing high school story like getting pantsed outside of chemistry class or showing up to school with toothpaste on your face. I still worry that you'll hear the story and think, You know, that group of hormonal high school jerkballs had a point—you *are* ugly. As if they still have power over me. But I know better now. Though sometimes I still take refuge in a comforting orange Creamsicle.

CHAPTER 4

When Fig Newtons Are the Last Straw

On Leaving Palm Springs

By the time I was ready to go to college, I had developed a well-crafted ideological position on Palm Springs, summed up by: *Palm Springs is the cultural armpit of America.*[1] I *had* to leave. I had a series of well-reasoned arguments on the nature of Palm Springs, presented here in bullet-point form:

---

1. Doesn't everyone think their hometown is the cultural armpit of America? Unless your hometown is Portland, in which case you think your hometown is the cultural capital of armpits...unwashed armpits. You know, because they're a bunch of dirty hippies (and now dirty hipsters).*
* WHOA! I just threw Portland under the bus for no reason. I actually love Portland (when it's not raining), and I've eaten multiple donuts there. Thank you, Portland.

A Young Woman's Philosophical Meditation on Palm Springs: The Bullet Points

- Every cactus prick on my fingers is like a pinprick on human development itself.
- The petite bourgeoisie of Palm Springs are too busy rewrapping their tennis rackets to notice the dissolution of their own humanity.
- My soul has withered in this dusty terrain, now please order me a hot dog on a stick *with* cheese. *Do not* forget the cheese.

These meditations on Palm Springs gave way to very real fears about a future in the golf-club-rich terrain of Southern California, which included the following:

A Young Woman's Fears About a Future in Southern California: The Bullet Points

- If I stay in the desert, my brain could turn into cactus jizz.
- I'll die at the Denny's, with a bunch of senior citizens who are also dying.
- I'll end up being one of those people who buys hand cream in bulk.
- What if I want a barista job that's not at a Starbucks? How am I supposed to grow as a barista?
- Inevitably someone will yell "Fore!" and inevitably I won't hear it and inevitably I'll get killed by a senior citizen with a shitty drive.

To make matters worse, my parents were like Guantanamo prison guards. Which is to say that they never let me *do anything.* I had more rules than any kid at school. Mind you, I was a perfect student with the best grades, which you think would mean I got more privileges. But that doesn't cut it for their immigrant work ethic. Being a perfect student is a total given. It's just what you're *supposed* to do.

How a Young Woman's Parents "Celebrated" Good Grades

☐ You got a perfect report card? That's great—how about you practice piano to celebrate?

☐ You were voted president of the debate club? Good. Why don't you clean up your room so it's more befitting of a president?

☐ You were just cast in a school play? Good—we just bought a stationary bike so you can exercise your excitement off.

☐ You received a scholarship to go to college? Here are some Fig Newtons.

Fig Newtons, bitches! You know what's really exciting about Fig Newtons? They're made from figs, and you know how kids go crazy over *figs*! Oh man, and that unsugary exterior? Wrap them dried-fruit delights up and pass them out as Christmas gifts, because it is *Fig Newtons* and not *chocolate* that people should give each other during times of celebration.

Growing up, my parents also couldn't wrap their heads around why I was *kinda chubby*. I wasn't super overweight, this wasn't a "let's call in the fire department with a crane" situation. But they were always suspicious.

Accusations Wielded by a Mother Toward Her Daughter

☐ Are you hiding chocolates under your bed?
☐ Are you hiding those colorful candies under your bed? (I think she meant Nerds/Runts/SweeTarts.)
☐ Are you hiding a McDonald's burger under your bed?

Yeah, I was asked, on multiple occasions, whether I was hiding a hamburger under my bed. You know, because hamburgers are the kind of thing that you can just put in a drawer and eat little by little. They hold up! Oh mother, the real trouble comes from hiding hamburgers in your body.[2]

And why did she think I always hid these things under my bed? I did not nor have I ever had a relationship with the under part of my bed. It collects dust. Occasionally I store sweaters under there. Moreover, I think we can all agree that it's lost its zest as the Great American Hiding Spot, because everyone looks under the bed first. So if I'm gonna hide anything, it wouldn't be *under the bed*. If I did want to hide something, I would throw it in an old-timey tin box in the top shelf of my closet or deep within my leg warmers drawer. Mind you, I was never accused of hiding drugs or alcohol. These were all food-based accusations.

---

2. To be fair, my kinda-chubby status confounded me, too. I wasn't that bad with the eating. My only explanation is that I grew up in the United States and a lot of us are kinda chubby. Maybe it's because our foods are made from malted thiamin monoglyceride mixed with hormones, and spiked with aspartame. I don't know, I'm just spitballin'.

I also hated Palm Springs because the Southern California lifestyle is based on car ownership. You have to drive and you must own a car or else. I'm pretty sure that's the state motto, but Google it before you quote me. I am what some might refer to as "a terrible driver." But honestly, it's not the driving but the parking that really gets me.

Like any red-blooded American teen with zits and a tendency to eye-roll, I got my driver's license at sixteen. I was a sophomore. My parents gave me a Honda Accord to drive around that was *from the '70s*. Since the car was older than me, they didn't really care what happened to it. I spent the next two years of my life scuffing it up in various parking accidents. There wasn't a parking lot bumper I didn't hit. There wasn't a parallel parking scenario that didn't agitate my gallstones. Here are things you would hear me say about these various parking mishaps:

A Young Woman Justifies Her Parking Mishaps

- □ I don't think it's normal for a parking garage to have such a narrow entrance.
- □ I don't know, I honestly thought I had enough room, but then I was suddenly on the sidewalk.
- □ You'd think a supermarket parking lot would design wider turns between lanes.
- □ I feel like this spot was meant for teleportation and not for actual driving.
- □ What am I supposed to do if the Rite Aid doesn't have a valet?

You know who I never blamed? This guy (I'm pointing at myself). I never blamed this guy.

So, between my antidesert rants, the Farsad dictatorship, and my endless parking nightmare, Palm Springs was dust. It was toast. It was goosed. It was cooked. It was burnt on one side and it would never taste good in these buns. It was time to go.

CHAPTER 5

A Protester Is Born

Dave Matthews, Pleated Khakis, and the Reverend Al Sharpton

College! It's where young and oversexed students formulate their *thinking* while getting small tattoos they can conceal from their parents and also adopting a much more lax hygiene regimen.

Just as I considered myself Mexican in high school, in college I began shifting my sights to being black (hopefully you read the introduction—but you may be reading this book in reverse order, in which case, carry on anyway). I started watching Spike Lee movies, critiqued academia's default Eurocentrity, and bemoaned the whiteness of shows like *Boy Meets World*. I presented my position through such bold acts as wearing a Malcolm X T-shirt on campus.

A bold act

I was a double major in government and theatre, which meant every political-science assignment was an opportunity to theatrically decry our society's racial divide. It also meant that I stage-managed the school's production of the one play they put on about slavery. For real.[1]

I was awash in the politics of neocolonialism; I would gleefully stump on the canon of Senegalese film; I joyfully

1. Sadly, I can't remember or figure out the name of the play, but the cast included about a dozen black actors: One white Jewish woman was cast to play a male slave owner, the director was black, and I stage-managed. The Jewish actor was both really pleased to be cast and really horrified at the same time. I just felt as if I was getting closer and closer to my purpose.

ranted on the inherent inequality of intergenerational wealth transfer. Basically, I was superfun at parties. It was a politically charged environment, and I poured my sociopolitical frustrations into blackness.

Race awareness hit me from the very first moments of college, even from my very first college friend. Molly was extremely well liked, blond, beautiful, friendly, funny, smart, and athletic, and to top it off, she could drop juicy gossip with the best of them. We lived in the same dorm freshman year and were instant besties. We were the inexplicably noisy neighbors amidst a large population of really shy and quiet people: "You're just walking to the kitchen, how are you so noisy??" *I don't know, it's a talent!*

Later in life, a downstairs neighbor who happened to be my landlord came to inspect my apartment one day. He asked if we had considered putting down any carpet and I said, "No way, have you seen the wood floors! To die!" And then he said, "Because you have a very heavy walk. It sounds like a bunch of rhinoceroses up here." My roommate nodded her head, "It's true. You have a heavy gait." As a girl who's been battling weight my whole life, I immediately Googled "how much do rhinos weigh." They can weigh up to five thousand pounds. I understood the rhino analogy to be an exaggeration and promised to wear slippers. But it's still hard not to think of myself as a loud, lone, rhino, clomping around the earth...in slippers. Molly was skinny, but she also had a rhino walk, which was what made us friends.

(Brought the story back to Molly despite a huge diversion

into rhinos! *Come on!* That's how you get segues done, bitches!)

Molly and I now have a drink once a year when she's in town, but one time, a couple of years ago, our meeting had a different vibe. I was wearing a weird outfit (shades of pink coupled with a green ascot, it was a quick judgment call, I don't have to defend myself to you!). Oh, and I was also slowly sipping on a Jägermeister because I was going through a "Jägermeister is actually a really good digestif" period, and look, it's not my job to defend the health benefits of Jägermeister, I'll let the next comedian do that, but it *does* calm a crazy stomach, so get off my back already! Point is, this meeting was different because Molly had *something to say*. At one point she broke down in tears, apologizing about her treatment of me and her roommate at Cornell.

Her roommate was Chinese-American. She grew up in New York City's Chinatown and had an overprotective family. She never experienced the all-American cheerleaders-and-popularity parade that Molly had. I was somewhere in between them. I think we were both a bit envious of what Molly got to grow up with—that is, uncomplicated whiteness. The endless sloppy joes, sleepovers, and press-on nails. To be clear, we both loved Molly, because she was lovable. But here was Molly, years later, crying at a bar to me because her freshman self didn't understand that there was a real difference between us, that we didn't have the same upbringing she did. That we didn't immediately fit in the way she always had. She hadn't understood cultural sensitivity or the privilege of dominance or what it felt like to never question belonging. She just got to put on the press-on nails and have a laugh.

She had all the benefits of being a mean girl without ever having been mean. She used her powers for good and not evil, because she was a fundamentally nice person. She never did anything terrible; she mostly just dragged me to frat parties where I wasn't quite welcome or made assumptions about our home lives, whether or not we ever had boyfriends or went to dances. Her assumptions weren't horrible, but they were only true for her particular white suburban upbringing. But the fact that she was crying only meant that she realized ten years later that she had lacked exposure. She hadn't been thoroughly groomed for this level of compassion. Having to consider another person's entirely different cultural context hadn't occurred to her before. She had been raised around people like her or people who knew to defer to her. That was what college was: It was like being around a bunch of people, some good, some bad, but most of them not yet groomed for this kind of compassion.

I went to Cornell University in upstate New York, and upon arrival I thought it was a foreign land, completely different from Southern California. First off, there were trees everywhere, lush, green ones I had seen only in movies. Second of all, there were basically no Mexicans as far as the eye could see. As the theory went, Mexicans went as far north as Poughkeepsie and stopped. They just didn't want to go any farther.

New York - The Empire State

I had never seen so many white people in my life. I remember thinking, Maybe I should try being white? I mean, what does it really entail—wainscoting? I can do that. But on my campus, the gatekeepers to whiteness were frat boys.

Despite its academic rigor, Cornell has a very entrenched Greek system. During my time there, white people were *extremely* concerned with it. They were willing to fake-kidnap people to get into fraternities, willing to stand naked and have their fat circled with Sharpies to get into sororities, willing to join a cappella groups. There was no amount of humiliation a white person wouldn't put up with to get into this Greek system! It was *very* important. The benefits were apparently *huge*.

NAMES BELONGING TO THE SORORITY GIRLS
(OF MY MIND)

- ☐ Kateland Bananaclip
- ☐ Burberry St. Cloud
- ☐ Morgan Van Tinkle of the Great Neck Van Tinkles
- ☐ Taylor "Feather" Bitsimmons
- ☐ Morgan Tannerfly
- ☐ Tanner Morganfly
- ☐ Mackenzie Sticks
- ☐ Lizzie Flatterly
- ☐ Jenny Cortland Wassterstein-Hudson
- ☐ Madison Doilybean
- ☐ Ashley Grandmolding
- ☐ Snowflake Tibbles (sister of Pantaloon Tibbles)
- ☐ Maggie McSnippens
- ☐ Veronica Boatsmooth
- ☐ Jackie Windsails
- ☐ Karen McMonogram
- ☐ Lilac Duster
- ☐ Jordan Periwinkle
- ☐ Capri Greystone

Basically, if you got into the Greek system, you got invited to all these parties where you got to meet all the other white people who had also humiliated themselves to get into the Greek system. You would then see these people all the time and you would make out or date or masturbate alone in adjacent rooms. You would live exclusively among each other, which usually meant around white people.[2] Full sorority houses would be matched up with full fraternity houses for mixers and if that mixer ended in a mild pseudo-rape situation, then congratulations, you totally did it right!

My first brush with the Greek system was in the first two weeks of my freshman year. I followed Molly and a group of blond newbies to a frat party, dressed in my outsider best—Nine Inch Nails T-shirt, flowy dark medieval skirt, army boots, dark burgundy lipstick, and, for ultimate confusion, dangly Iranian earrings. Our frat hosts were wearing baseball caps and flip-flops, and button-down shirts that weren't tucked in; some of them had T-shirts inexplicably hanging out of their back pockets. Occasionally, there was a polo shirt.

I walked into the party thinking, I can pass, but when the full scale of the whiteness hit me, I realized passing wasn't my choice. I didn't get to choose whiteness. You're *rewarded* whiteness.

In my school, the rewards for that whiteness were doled out at frat parties. The blond girls with me were immediately branded for potential boning, so they were given beers and a tour of the premises. I was left to fend for myself while fighting my way into the keg line. Despite my sizable rack, I was not branded. No white-boy boning for me. Whiteness was beginning to look extremely unap-

---

2. To be fair, we also had one or two Jewish sororities/fraternities and a black fraternity that I can remember.

NAMES BELONGING TO THE SORORITY GIRLS
(CONT'D)

☐ Selena Ploughbow
☐ 'Nessa Crabtree
☐ Heather McKinKin
☐ Britt Marble
☐ Brittany Unicom
☐ Abigail Pincenez
☐ Holly Chateaubriand
☐ Geraldine Saddles
☐ Charlotte Chesapeake
☐ Allison Cufflinks
☐ Joni Habbidash
☐ Missy Winslet
☐ Cupcake Livingston
☐ Evangeline Townsend
☐ Lior Goldbergberg (Jewish sorority)
☐ Ambrosia Buchanan
☐ Summer Winterly
☐ Olivia Hornswaddle
☐ Claire Binghampton
☐ Courtney Bing-Hampton
☐ Langley Pleats
☐ Cheyanne "Throw Pillow" Templeton

---

pealing. (I mean, I had to lose my V *eventually*, and if I couldn't get any play at white parties, how was *that* gonna happen?) I thought I'd at least get some kind of weird frat-boy fetishist who thought my features were exotic or something. But no. I fought to get my one beer and ended up walking back to the dorm alone, like a straight coat-check girl who'd just finished her shift at a gay bar.

As school started in earnest, I also discovered that whiteness involved a deep and abiding commitment to Dave Matthews. Well, that was just asking too much. There's no way me and my Björk CD collection could join. Not that it mattered, because I couldn't pass anyway.

But Cornell had its own racial issues a brewin', and I just happened to be there at the right time to get mobilized by them. You see, part of the reason Molly was so noticeable in my dorm was that she was a sorority-bound white girl and we didn't have those in Low Rise 7. Low Rise 7 was the name of our dorm, but others were called stuff like Baker Tower, named after a notable moneybags alum. At Cornell, there were a select few of us (hundreds of us) in these less savory, less popular dorms with really functional names and numbers and very little class spirit. Hey, at least we weren't Low Rise 9—they were the *last* of the practically named Low Rises. How embarrassing.

Class spirit was spread very unevenly on our beautiful campus at that time. This was mainly because incoming freshmen got to select where they lived. We each handed in a form over the summer with our top three dorm choices, and we generally got one of those dorms. Seems simple enough. But the result was: West Campus had most of the white people, and all the people of color ended up on North Campus. Separate but equal.

Cornell was big on legacy. Fathers wanted their sons

A PROTESTER IS BORN 89

to join the same fraternity. Mothers wanted their daughters to join the same lacrosse team. Multiple generations would graduate from Cornell, and because this dates back decades, all of them were white. Even if their parents didn't have Cornell credentials, they went to top-tier universities, sent their kids to the best private schools, and had remarkable connections. These incoming legacy students had more information on Cornell. They could ask a relative or a connected family friend, "Hey, what dorms should I rank?" and those contacts would say, "The dorms on West Campus." And then they would say "What are your thoughts on pleated khakis?" and the family friend would say, "I'm pro, very pro pleated khakis."

WHAT THE CAMPUS ELITE DID ON PARENTS WEEKEND

- ☐ Manage orchids
- ☐ Train parakeets
- ☐ Wear little tennis outfits to brunch
- ☐ Procure season-specific monogrammed umbrellas
- ☐ Attend secret underground skin-care societies
- ☐ Tailor various trousers
- ☐ Hold private monthly conference calls with Kelsey Grammer
- ☐ Do weight test comparisons of precious metals
- ☐ Design customized watch bands
- ☐ Get drunk

Me, I knew one guy. The brother of my one Iranian friend in high school went to Cornell. I asked him where to live and he said, "I don't know, I lived in North Campus." No shit you lived in North Campus—you were a minority!

But see, so many of the white students ranked West Campus that not everyone got their wish. So, people like Molly slipped through the cracks and ended up in a North Campus dorm with a Chinese-American roommate and an Iranian-American bestie. Most of these students tried to transfer out of these lame loser dorms. Others just waited it out until they could pledge a sorority/fraternity and be reunited with their people.

I lived next to the Ujamaa house, so I interacted with black students all the time. Plus I had two Indians and a Latina in my suite, and then there was Molly and her Chinese-American roommate down the hall, so I was getting the full spectrum of diversity. Basically, the people of color were doing great at meeting people of color. The white students were doing great at listening to Dave Matthews.

To Cornell's credit, they did place some kind of multicultural half floor of a dorm on West Campus. So about a few dozen out of several hundred students on West Campus were minorities. But that wasn't enough, because eventually tensions flared.

In response to the segregation, Cornell thought that first-year residents should not be allowed to live in "program housing." For example, African-Americans who wanted to live in the Ujamaa Residential College, a program house dedicated to "the rich and diverse heritage of Black people in the United States, Africa, the Caribbean, and other regions of the world," would be prohibited from doing so as first-year students. But program houses were the de facto centers of racial identity. It almost seemed like the university wanted to reduce their presence on campus by limiting the number of people who could live in them. It was as if they wanted these centers of identity—these places where black, Latino, and Native American students felt at home, felt a sense belonging—to eventually die off.

My friend Anyeley, a Ghanaian-American salsa addict, was the minority liaison to the administration at the time. She remembers trying to get the administration to listen to her. She felt frustrated with their questions, with the fact that they didn't understand what program houses meant to her fellow students. She felt so defeated in her dealings with the university that at one point she cried in a committee meeting. A photo of her crying made it to the campus newspaper. She cried because she was nineteen with erratic emotions. *But* she also cried because she didn't want the university to take away the program houses where minorities like her got to let down their guards and just be. Molly would cry years later when this kind of distinction finally made sense to her. Have you ever worn Spanx all day and you come home, take off the Spanx, and let your gut hang out? Being a person of color on campus all day is like wearing Spanx, and a program house is where you let your gut hang out with no shame.[3]

Then Al Sharpton drove up to campus to say, "Nuh-uh." That's right, the West Campus–North Campus divide got to be so bad, and the university's response was so wrong-headed that student-organized marches across campus were joined by marching royalty Al Sharpton! He thought the university's plan was ridiculous and mocked it: "We want more blacks and Latinos on campus; we just want them to merge with everyone else so we don't know they're here."[4] He was right. The university's panties were in a bunch over the wrong thing. Only 1.4 percent of students lived in those program houses. They weren't the real problem.

Looking back on it, it was disgusting that Cornell let this unofficial separation exist. How could they not see the generational and racial effects of these dorm selections? But schools like Cornell were so old that it took them a little time, a little marching, and a lot of Al Sharpton, to figure out what was going wrong on campus.

This incident on our campus was *huge* for us students. We were all vim and vigor and ready to march and get angry. Some students even staged hunger strikes. I did not. But I did take advantage of the seemingly endless

---

3. Obviously, changing the social divide on campus was much much more important than Spanx, but not all analogies are perfect.

4. Weird! A footnote that is actually intended to give you bibliographic information: Michael Bocian, "Housing on College Campuses," U.S. Department of Education, Institute of Education Sciences, http://files.eric.ed.gov/fulltext/ED446596.pdf.

supply of seasoned curly fries, and I was extraordinarily devoted to the Sweet Rachel[5] sandwich at Collegetown Bagel.

But I did march. And I...felt things. I had little pangs of anger. I looked upon the old men that ruled the school and realized that they had huge blind spots. That they alone couldn't possibly be the answer to our school's segregation problem. That without us—the marchers of color—there would be no fair solution.

To the school's credit, they changed their policies, and dorm selection was randomized while maintaining program housing. The face of the entire campus changed.

That experience made me aware of race, and I never did look back. Once you see the racial divide, you can't unsee it. Cornell made me into a protester. And you know what? Eventually I did buy a Dave Matthews CD. I'm human, after all. I'm happy to report that there are now more Mollys hanging out with more Negins. As it should be.

---

5. A warm and delicious sandwich of turkey, Muenster cheese, honey mustard, and lettuce on pumpernickel bread. The honey mustard was special, and I have not seen the likes of it in non-Collegetown bagel establishments.

CHAPTER 6

My Lady Parts and
My Comedy Parts

The struggle of holding a protest sign in the cold, followed by the act of getting a hot chocolate at Collegetown Bagel, did a great job of politicizing me and activating my burning desire for hot chocolate. (Did I mention that protesting in the cold was...cold?)

But while that was going on, I was also in the throes of another hot burning desire: comedy. Who said you can't love two things at the same time? *You can.* And it can really complicate your academic schedule.

I was hooked on acting in high school. But I assumed that interest, along with my acne, would fade by the time I was in a serious academic setting. Oh Negin, you naïve little co-ed. Thinking that an interest would fade just because school was absurdly expensive. Thinking that an Interest in comedy would simply vanish because you didn't want to disappoint your parents by studying something so buffoon-like and self-serving. Did you know that your Interests don't give a rat's butt about tuition? No, they don't. Did you know that your Interests couldn't give a flying fuck about "career stability"? No, they don't give a fuck—a flying or an earthbound fuck. Your Interests are a great big bag of dicks. And they're ready to bone.

For some people, Interests align with financially sound and respectable career choices, and for other people, quite sadly, they don't. Interests scream loudly in some people's heads, creating their own mosh pit like at some '90s grunge concert. And for others, they're weak piddly little flirtations that have virtually no lumbar support. My Interests gave me tinnitus—instead of a ringing in the ear it was the voice of Lewis Black yelling, *Fucking go into comedy you fuck*. And then I would see a vein on Lewis Black's head pop.

During the First Year Orientation show in that first week of college, I was a goner. The show was designed to woo the horribly awkward freshman—freshman so fresh we still wore our high school theatre company and track team T-shirts. The performing groups wanted us to become their new fans or audition for their open slots, that kind of thing. There were a dangerously large number of a cappella groups performing. A cappella groups are both totally entertaining and an embarrassment to all of humanity. A cappella is like a really juicy episode of *Real Housewives of Atlanta*, a show you pretend you know nothing about but secretly watch.[1] Enjoying a cappella is like that rare moment when you're alone ordering a pizza—as in an entire pizza for yourself—and you get to say, "Extra cheese, please," and the pizza shop guy is like, "Well, that's not an option," and you're like, "I'll pay you whatever you want, just give me double the amount of cheese," and the guy is like, "Okay, fine." You hang up the phone and you're extremely satisfied with your order, because you can never admit to doing shit like that with your friends around, when you have to pretend like you're the kind of person that never has even ever considered ordering double the cheese on a pizza. That's what enjoying a cappella is like.

So there I was sitting in an auditorium with my faux-indifferent posture, like the first week of college was no big deal. I clapped and yawned as the multitudinous a cappella groups sang pop songs from the likes of James Taylor, when finally it was time for the show-stopping sketch comedy troupe: the Skits-o-Phrenics. Let's just put the name aside for a second to say that they were *good*. To my little far-sighted eyes they seemed better than *Saturday Night Live*! They made me laugh from all cylinders and with scant attention to cackling. I looked upon that stage from the mezzanine level and said, "as God is my witness, I will join that sketch comedy troupe." I said it just like that, with a fist in the air, and a thick Shakespearian affect.

I was in college, with no intention of comedy shenani-

---

1. Oh, for the record, I don't watch *Real Housewives*…Of course, I *would* say that.

gans. But just when I thought I was out, my Interests kept pulling me back in. Yeah, in this analogy, comedy is like the mob and it kills people.[2]

I did in fact audition for (and got into) the Skits-o-Phrenics, and by the third week of school I was a full-fledged member. I found out because they showed up to my dorm in the middle of the night with a bottle of Boone's wine and a pack of Ring Dings. That was how they haze-announced that you got into the group. It was very classy.

Those motherfuckers kept the Interest alive, kept it chomping at the bit, and I became a sketch comedy machine. As a freshman in college, comedy was tied in first place (along with "fighting for the struggle") as the most important thing in my as-yet-inconsequential life.

And it was good I found comedy and politics, because Cornell wasn't exactly an obvious fit for me. I discovered very soon after I got there that I didn't like nature very much, and Cornell had a lot of trees. So many trees. Nature was everywhere, all these little bits of it, little brooks and gorges.[3] Any walk from dorm to class or from class to dining hall involved some kind of grassy, steep, death-defying hill. Students wore hiking boots to class. Everyone had grappling hooks dangling off their backpacks and they really valued their fleece. I hated all of that. I never wanted to be rugged, or strenuously exercised, or a little cold. I wanted to put on my black lipstick

---

2. Comedy *is* like the mob and it *does* kill people.
3. Have you seen someone wearing the "Ithaca is Gorges" T-shirt? The "Ithaca is Gorges" T-shirt is to Ithaca what the "YOLO" T-shirts were to 2013. Everyone has one, we're all embarrassed about it.

and go to a café with my Sartre compendium. You know, like a normal person. Of course, if I wasn't at a café looking morose, I was doing comedy.

I would spend hours and hours rehearsing comedy. I would poster the campus walls with our show flyers promoting comedy. I would develop accents, design props, and figure out the best way to tromp around the stage in character performing comedy. The one thing that I resisted for a long time was writing comedy.[4]

Here's why: I was one of two women in a group of about twelve guys. I was convinced that I wasn't a good writer. To be a good writer meant that I had to be smart. And I was convinced that I wasn't smart. I'm still not entirely convinced otherwise, but now I recognize that it's stupid to think that you're stupid. A lot of women actually feel like this—we're socialized to somehow think we're big, fat frauds when in fact we're overcompensating go-getters.

Ugh, how many times have you heard a lady say, "Oh, I'm not qualified for this" or "I don't really know what I'm doing" or "I'm not sure this PhD means very much." Come on! You've heard it a million times. I just wanna grab those ladies and say, "Turn your vagina down, get in there, and don't let those nutsacks talk over you. And when you're done, demand that the air-conditioning be turned off, because why do we have to work in a refrigerator because some guy gets the occasional pit stain???"

Of course, the male-female divide isn't all in our heads.

---

4. We're talking a whole six months, which in college is like "a long time."

When you look at the top 100 highest grossing films of 2013/2014, only 2 percent were directed by women![5] That's a single digit—in fact, it's the first single digital after the first single digit. It's a low-ass digit. That's just in my business. In the tech world, only 26 percent of U.S. computing jobs were held by women in 2013.[6] So the lacking confidence in your head meets the actual crappy statistics in real life—the "craptistics"—and then voilà! A lady feels bad and then sees doom and then feels bad again in a horrible loop that's being held together by pantyhose.

That loop worked hard in my brain tentacles. I resisted writing until I realized that the parts I was getting from the boys were, in a word, dogshit. There was the "dumb sorority girl"[7] or the "nagging housewife,"[8] or my personal favorite, the "woman standing in corner." It wasn't long before I exhausted every nagging voice I could think of, and every dumb sorority girl nuance I could eke out, and every standing pose available to a bipedal mammal. If I wanted to do something about the comedic parts I was playing, I had to write them myself. I started teaming up with peeps in the group to ease my way into writing.

---

5. http://mobile.nytimes.com/2015/05/13/movies/aclu-citing-bias-against
-women-wants-inquiry-into-hollywoods-hiring-practices.html?_r=0.
6. Emily Peck, "The Stats on Women in Tech Are Actually Getting Worse," *Huffington Post*, March 27, 2015, http://www.huffingtonpost
.com/2015/03/27/women-in-tech_n_6955940.html.
7. In a school composed entirely of straight-A students we thought we had "dumb girls." We didn't.
8. Yes, as college students we had remarkable insight on how marriage worked.

Some of those guys would be lifelong friends, collaborators, and recipients of my mass e-mails.

I started with writing superhero, video game, and fart-based materials. I wanted to blend in, I wanted to be one of the boyzzz. Sometimes I would write a *female* superhero character that just ended up being androgynous.[9] Frankly, I didn't know how to write a female character that was in a position of power. I just hadn't seen very many of those. So when I thought about a corporate office sketch with a bunch of CEO characters being you know, "hilarious," the way CEOs are, all the men around the table were white, with erectile dysfunction. If it was a sketch about an ad agency coming up with "hilarious" commercials, the leader of the group was always a guy.

But college was all about learning how to make a stink. So, I started to make a stink about the lady characters in our sketches. I started challenging the boys in the group on their casting and their narrow vision of women in sketches. They weren't always sensitive to where I stood, but that was only because they'd never encountered the issue before. I was probably the first person in their young lives who said, "Instead of two men, why can't we show two female baseball fans making fools of themselves?" Or "Why can't I, a woman, play a male president and wear a man's suit? Guys play women all the time. I mean, Milton Berle built a whole career on it, right?"

---

9. In the interest of accuracy, this particular superhero sketch was about a series of dining hall vegetables that saved college students from doom. I'm in talks with Marvel to turn it into a movie franchise starring Charlize Theron in the role of the Rapacious Rutabaga.

There were battles, there were laughs, there was an awakening of my tits. But I was really naïve about the makeup of the group, worried that if we brought any more women into the group, I would have fewer and fewer parts. I operated from a "glass is half empty...of vaginas" philosophy. I was shameful and I was scared. The opportunities for me, even in that idealistic college situation, looked so scarce. Everywhere I turned in my limited little comedy world I saw white dudes with brown hair and glasses. We even had a sketch lampooning the sheer number of them we had in our group called "White Dudes with Brown Hair and Glasses."

Sometimes it still looks scarce, but the answer should never be: *Get me in there and keep all of them other ladies out!* What was it that Madeleine Albright said? I think she said something like "There's a special circle of hell reserved for women who don't help other women," or maybe she said, "There's an especially terrible sketch with no speaking parts for female actor/comedians who don't help other female actor/comedians."

Years later, I was on *The Nightly Show with Larry Wilmore* on Comedy Central. At the end of each show, each panelist gets asked one of those catch-22-type questions. If the host—the indomitable Larry Wilmore—thinks that your answer is sincere, he awards you a *Keeping It 100* card (like keeping it 100 percent real, for those of you who don't speak street). The question for me: If you could definitely eradicate one of these things—but not both— would you eradicate Islamophobia or Sexism?

I said Sexism. I cited my mother—she was the first thing that came to mind. That shit affected my mother and it's

still around! We can't have that! Besides, all women suffer
from sexism—if we get rid of that, we could free up the
white ladies to fight against Islamophobia, right? Newly
freed-up white ladies would make wonderful allies for all
kinds of fights if they didn't have to deal with sexism.
Imagine the possibilities!

The fight in being a woman and the fight in being a
person of color is the same fight, but being a woman *and*
a person of color just adds twelve extra steps. Like you
can make a turkey for Christmas dinner, or you can make
things real hard for yourself and go for the turducken.
Going for the turducken isn't easy; for starters, you have
to debone three separate birds. What a nightmare! And

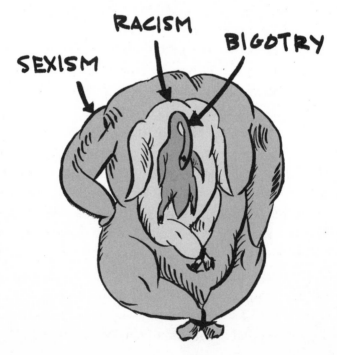

to pull that off at Christmas dinner? Being a woman of color is like always going for the turducken. I believe Gertrude Stein used the same analogy.

It was in this little microuniverse of gendered politics, protected by the low stakes of college sketch comedy, where I figured out that I wanted to have my lady parts and my comedy, too. And cake, I really wanted cake. Throughout college, my Interests definitely had their way. They boned me real hard. And thank God, because I wouldn't have started writing without them.

CHAPTER 7

Bootleg Islam

One of my tried-and-true methods of making white people laugh—or you know, having a pleasant connected chat—is describing my experiences with family, especially family in Iran. People tend to find it fascinating. They're surprised to learn that Iranian life is equal parts humdrum and repressive. They're amazed to learn that neuroses strike mothers of all races, ethnicities, and faiths uniformly. They ask questions about the food and the scenery, the clothes and the customs. At first I didn't share much of this stuff, because I thought it was common knowledge, like I would bore people. You might not tell me every detail of a trip to your aunt's house because you think it might bore me (or worse yet, bore you as you're talking about it). But how wrong I was! Because family gripes are the great connector, they're the foundation of 93 percent of all comedians' careers, and they are the ultimate social lubricant.

Sometimes I find myself telling people about a particular trip I took to Iran, soon after I moved to New York
City. I went there for my cousin's wedding. This was the
first time I would be traveling to the Islamic Republic
of Iran on my own. Up until my eighteenth birthday I
had always traveled with my mom. My dad and brother
never came with us, because they feared being drafted
into military service. For Iranian males, military service
is mandatory, and even though my brother was an American citizen, the Iranian government, like honey badger,
don't care. Which is to say, because he was born in Iran
to an Iranian father, Iran will always have citizenship
eyes for him. Whenever he walks into a room, Iran will
always blush. If he ever calls collect, Iran will always
accept the charges. Citizenship in Iran is forever, even if
the person has totally moved on, is seeing another country, or is even totally *citizened* to another country! This
makes Iran a stalkery ex. What it has meant for my dad
and brother is that they weren't able to go back until well
after military age.

But me and Moms did go, because this was the very
very rare moment where being a woman actually gave us
more freedom. We would spend long summer months in
Iran. Our family would throw hundreds of parties, give
us tons of gifts, like handcrafted little Persian rug mouse
pads and jewelry boxes with ancient Iranian designs.
These things cost a ton at Pottery Barn but you can get
them for a dime in Iran. My point is, the whole country
is a great shopping experience.

My second point is, the whole country is filled with

party hosts. These people love throwing parties. If there was an Olympics game for teatime, Iran would not only take home the gold, but the Olympics committee would create some kind of new metal—the Platinum Titanium Deluxe—and then Iran would take that home, too. I know you think the British are supposed to be the undisputed leaders of teatime, but that's only because America has better relations with the Brits and have thus popularized their teatime traditions. In Iran, teatime is *constant*, and it's *everywhere*. If you go shopping for clothes, you're offered tea and pastries. If you're visiting someone at the hospital, a magical elf appears offering tea and pastries. There's tea service in prisons. You can rap on a neighbor's door, ask for a spare extension cord, and *bam*, there's a tea set just waiting for you. They anticipate your extension cord needs and have three forms of pastries waiting *just in case*.

They're not just good hosts; they insist on making you feel kingly. First there's the hellos. In the United States, we walk into someone's home and we're likely to say something like "Hey, how are you? I love your place! Thanks for having me." And then the host will say something like "Oh thanks, so glad you could make it." That's about the size of the hellos. But in Iran, the hellos start with the recitation of a couple of ancient poems, probably from Rūmī. There might be a quick nod to some kind of more modern sonnet, topped off by a couple of platonic epistemologies on the nature of having a guest. They like to start with a solid, discursive foundation.

Then, the hosts looks at you—I mean really looks at

you. They breathe you in and then they offer a thousand blessings. I never know how to respond, so I usually offer two thousand blessings in return. They take those two thousand blessings and raise me. Soon we're jumping up to ten thousand blessings. I don't want to shy away from this. What am I, a pussy? I can do more than ten thousand on a bad day. I just go for it. I say, "I wish upon you *one million blessings*." In most Western societies, this is more blessings than is strictly comfortable for the average person. But in Iran, they go full-hog "infinite blessings," and then you know you're a goner. You're so fucking blessed, you don't know how to take your upcoming tea.

So after the twenty minutes' worth of hellos in the form of poems, blessings, and a healthy debate on the nature of greetings, you move into the sitting room. Not unlike their American counterparts, these sitting rooms are covered in plastic until you, a very important guest, can luxuriate your behind in the soft cushions of the Louis XIV imitation couch. That's when the tea comes out—there's no question if you would have a tea, it's just forced upon you. You wouldn't be able to say, "Oh, I'm off the caffeine, no thank you." I imagine you would just be banished from human society if you did that. So the tea is a must. But then come the pastries.

When it comes to the delivery of pastries, Iranians move like those high-speed vampires. They take out the good china, and before you're even able to comprehend physical movement, you're eating fresh almond cookies and baklava. They have to act fast because those almond cookies are *fresh*. Have you ever eaten a fresh almond cookie? It melts in your mouth. *No!* It melts on contact with your lips. You're probably really fond of an almond cookie you had in Chinatown or something, but lemme tell you—that almond cookie don't know shit. I don't mean to start a new war in Asia, but those Chinese almond cookies taste like paint sticks compared to the transcendent almond cookies of Iran.[1]

You can't have just one cookie. That's when the Iranian host activates the age-old tradition of *tarof*. Tarof goes like this:

Host: Please, have another cookie.
Guest: No, thank you. I'm full.
Host: Don't be ridiculous, have another cookie, you
　　　look like you're going to starve.
Guest: No, I'm fine, really thanks.
Host: I woke up at 5 A.M. to go to the bakery, to stand
　　　there before it opened, to ensure that you were get-
　　　ting a fresh almond cookie delivery, and I waited
　　　for three hours until it opened so I could buy the
　　　very first, the very freshest, batch of almond cook-
　　　ies, *for you*. Only *for you*. You must have another.
Guest: No, really, I'm good, thanks.
Host: I'll slice my own throat if you don't have another
　　　almond cookie, it is the most fresh and delicious
　　　almond cookie in all of Iran.

---

1. They're called *ghorabiye*—with the guttural *gh* sound that makes it sound like you're swallowing your face.

Guest: Okay...okay...put the butter knife down. I'll take another cookie.

Host: And another baklava?

Guest: Gah!

That's tarof. Sometimes it turns into a psychological thriller, but mostly Iranians want to make sure they treat you real nice and that you're stuffed by the time you leave. They are aggressively hospitable. Which is why their international reputation of being uncompromising on nuclear proliferation has never made sense to me.

So I always had fun in Iran. To have access to dozens of cousins and aunts and uncles and great-aunts and grandmothers gave me a sense of belonging.

I had always traveled with my mother. She always had a chador-type thing on hand for when we entered the Islamic Republic. Oh, I should probably explain: chadors are those long pieces of fabric, of any color, that women in Islamic countries drape over themselves. It's not a burka; you don't cover your face, you just drape this piece of fabric over your head, and hold it under your chin. Chadors are perfect for those moments when you're in an Islamic Republic and you just have to run out of the apartment and grab some milk from the corner store, but you don't feel like putting your arms into sleeves. Catholics may recognize the similarity between chadors and a nun habit. Tourists in London may recognize their similarity to the plastic poncho that the tour guide gives you in case it starts raining and you're on the second story of a double-decker bus.

In fact, there are a lot of covering-up rules in Iran.
Here are some of the basics:

☐ Ladies, you gotta cover your hair! Don't let that
   shiny mane out for everyone to see like some sort
   of slut. You gotta cover that shit up! It's the law.
☐ Ladies, you gotta cover the contours of your body.
   Don't let everyone see that slim waistline like some
   sort of slut. You gotta cover that shit up! It's the law.
☐ Gentlemen, you gotta cover those shoulders up! You
   can't wear wife beaters out in public like some sort
   of slut. You gotta cover that shit up! It's the law.

So there are some personal coverage issues, the burden
of which is shouldered mostly by the hot ladeez. But there
were other fun laws like: Alcohol is banned, and anything
from the West is considered contraband. So keeping these
rules in mind, I had to take care of a few things before
I traveled to Iran. My mother wouldn't be traveling with
me this time, so first, the *hijab*.

Hijab is the set of clothes that conforms with the Muslim
notion of modesty. But to be clear, for most Muslims that
definition is usually up to the ladies themselves. There are
plenty of Muslim countries, let's say Lebanon, that don't
have the hijab codified into law. Iran requires the hijab, but
still its definition of modesty is subjective and it changes
with the seasons. Literally, when it's warmer, sometimes,
they're a little looser on what constitutes proper hijab. You
could go out with your headscarf fully exposing fabulous
bangs or three-quarter sleeves on your long jacket. You

might see some wrists up in there! I should note though that even Koranic scholars themselves can't agree on how to interpret the concept of the hijab. Basically, the whole head-covering thing gets a lot of attention for what it says or doesn't say about Islam and women.

My grandmother covered whenever she was in the United States; it made her feel more comfortable. It never bothered me that she covered, and I didn't think it made her less of a feminist. In fact, it was my grandmother, not my grandfather, who clearly ran shit. We needed *her* approval on things. She had the intensity of a Queen Mother character you might see in *Game of Thrones*. Sure, her son or husband are technically the kings, but she's the one that's telling the Master of Coin how to negotiate trade agreements with the Warden of the North. She's the one who put a bounty on her dwarf brother's head via raven! My grandmother was a lovely person, so she never actually put a bounty on anyone's head, but she could have if she wanted! What's more, she never proselytized. She never tried to get anyone in her family to be more or less Muslim. For her the degree of involvement in Islam—the chadors, the prayer, the eating—was strictly opt-in. Do it if you want, let's not make a fuss. She was a woman with agency, and she chose to cover up in the U.S. when she didn't have to. It made her feel better. Just like high-waisted underwear make me feel better. And now you know.

But for women in Iran, it's legally sanctioned. So, I had to get myself some Islamic headgear. My first instinct was to go to Macy's. I asked if there was some sort of

"Muslim section" of the store. It is, after all, the world's largest department store. The saleswoman at Macy's was stumped. There were no Muslim outfits to be found so instead she showed me some really frilly and diaphanous scarves. I thought I should wear a thicker and more dour fabric, just to be safe, so I ended up buying a navy blue bed sheet from the Martha Stewart collection at Kmart. I figured the mullahs wouldn't mind 120-thread count.

Armed with my bedsheet hijab, I got on a plane and landed in Tehran. The first thing I noticed was that Tehran is hot and sweaty. And, don't get me wrong, I'm from the desert of Southern California, and at a very basic level I understood the *heat*. But what I didn't understand was wearing fifteen layers of clothing in ninety-five-degree weather with 60 percent humidity in the name of Islam.

The second thing I noticed was an earthquake that registered 7.0 on the Richter scale. And, don't get me wrong—I'm from the desert of Southern California, and at a very basic level I understand *earthquakes*. But what I didn't understand was that in Iran all the lights go out, buildings collapse, and people actually die. This never happened when we had 7.0s in Palm Springs. I have a T-shirt claiming survival from an earthquake from which *everyone* survived.

What are the odds! An earthquake right after I get off the plane? The earthquake happened right as I was about to go through customs. But as I walked in the lights went out and everybody started randomly running, so I started randomly running... The airport smelled like sweat...and enriched uranium.[2] It was the first night of the World Cup and some exotic country was playing another exotic country and airport staff was all up on that shit. The TVs went blank from the earthquake just as a ball was about to make a point but probably didn't, because there are no points in soccer-football.

Customs is a very intimate process in which the cultural police feel you up and go through your suitcase to find contraband. Getting searched was nerve-racking for me because I was, indeed, carrying contraband. Of course, in the United States we think of contraband as "drugs and weapons," but in Iran, my contraband was Jay Z albums and *Vogue* magazines. I really wanted to show my cousins that I was a hip purveyor of taste. Smuggling in this media was important in maintaining my family reputation as "the cool American cousin."

The lights had come back on, but the earthquake had rattled the cultural police, and they started phoning it in on the searches. As a result, the Sisters—or the female police force—didn't fondle my person too heavily (I had a CD tucked in my jacket). When it got to my suitcase, they asked me where I was from. I told them I was traveling from New York, they asked me a few more friendly questions. Apparently, my odd almost-American-clearly-bilingual-but-weird accent in Farsi was *the most adorable thing*. The accent got me free pastries and free trinkets, and in this case, it made me a successful smuggler of the complete Jay Z oeuvre.

---

2. Oh come on! I kid, of course it doesn't smell like enriched uranium.

The third thing I noticed was no less than one thousand family members waiting outside and shouting from all directions. Get this: They were ululating. Don't get me wrong: I live in the East Village of New York City, and I understand howling boys looking for a last-minute hookup before the bars close at 4 A.M. But what I didn't understand was that my family ululated out of elation because they were so happy to see me. If you've never made an entrance to ululation, I'm really sad for you. It is a singular wonder! I'm talking a bunch of auntlike ladies ululating at the top of their lungs, with a bunch of uncle types clapping and whistling in support. I don't see this kind of joy on display in my regular life, which makes me think I'm doing regular life all wrong.

Of course, that "cool American cousin" feeling quickly dissipated when they fully saw what I was wearing. There's a special feeling of embarrassment you get when you walk into a crowd of fashion forward chadors and you're wearing a bedsheet. I hadn't even cut off the tags. The horror.

I was there for my cousin's wedding. We were the same age, but I was a little nervous about hanging out with her and her sister. My life was different. I dated boys, drank alcohol, went to brunch, and actively took advantage of "the right of the people peaceably to assemble, and to petition the Government for a redress of grievances." None of these are huge in Iran, if we're being honest. I worried that out of the American context, my cousins would consider me some kind of

Iranian-American-slut-whore-hooker-prostitute, which, in New York we just call a Facebook friend.

But in many ways, my fears were unwarranted, because Iranians have the Islamic Republic figured out. They know how to live within the confines of a repressive regime. This is not a people to feel sorry for, and in fact Iran isn't the worst example of repression. Iranian women, for example, are a majority of college degree earners—that must not only make for lopsided college mixers, but it also means they end up being a meaningful chunk of the labor force. Iranian women can drive, unlike the ladies of Saudi Arabia. They can vote, they can go to libraries any time they want. There is a vibrant civic life in Iran. There are filmmakers, writers, and musicians. True, Taylor Swift will not be allowed to do a tour stop in Shiraz, but the image we might have of a bunch of sad Iranians crying that they can't publicly buy Beyoncé's feminist T-shirts, well, that's just not true.

It's not true, in part because Iranians are somehow able to import nearly any kind of contraband. I wasn't the only person bringing illegal music into the country. Everyone can get their hands on anything. Including alcohol. Lots of bootleg alcohol. My family aren't big drinkers and they're scaredy-cats, so they keep everything legal. But through friends of friends, I managed to get some bootleg gin. Did I get drunk on gin someone made in a bathtub? Yes. Yes I did. But you can also get regular beers and whatnot, smuggled in from Turkey. Everyone's got a guy. It's a lot like prohibition era United States, it's like the roaring 1320s over there.

Of course, I don't mean to paint too rosy a picture. Repression is in the air. At one point I was walking down the street with an aunt and I started whistling. Not to brag, but I have a fairly remarkable whistle which would, if needed, beat anyone else's whistle in a whistle-to-the-death-match scenario. A Lauryn Hill song popped into my head and I started whistling. Frankly, I was killing it when my aunt punched me in the arm. At first I thought she was shocked by my rock-hard whistling techniques. But it turned out she didn't want me to get arrested by the cultural police for whistling a Western tune in public.

I thought she was exaggerating. You can't police the micro stuff! And they generally don't. But there are occasions where they do. I was wearing a pair of sunglasses, a cheap plastic pair I got from a street vendor in New York for five dolla, five dolla! As I was walking down the street, a Sister, casually holding some sort of weapon, asked me to take off my glasses. She pointed out that they were "too fashionable." Yes, I was literally stopped by the Fashion Police. Except in Iran the Fashion Police carry assault rifles. I was pissing my chador. I have never been stopped by a cop before, so I suddenly felt like I was a fugitive from the law. I told her I understood and put the glasses in my purse. Upside: My fashionable American self just can't help but poke through. Downside: It's illegal to be that fashionable in Iran.

So the repression is real. But it's different in different countries, and I implore you, I beseech you, I beg of you to learn the differences before making snap judgments about this region. And don't wear sunglasses if you're ever in Iran. Just squint it out—it's not worth the hassle.

My cousin was getting married to a man she had met at work. She is an architect, and so was her Iranian crush. They flirted, dated, he popped the question, she agreed, a union was formed. Some of you will be surprised to learn that this was not an arranged marriage and that they both had graduate degrees. There were no camels involved, there were no snake charmers, there was no fat gentleman flying around on a rug granting people wishes. It was a meet-cute, courtship, and wedding. They might as well have been living in Sheboygan, it was so normsies.

But the wedding itself was cut straight from the traditional cloth of ancient Persia. Persian culture is what historians call "very old." The ethnically Persian peoples have inhabited that area in some form or another since 1500 BC. Their control of the region ran the gamut from defensively running shit, to preeminently running shit, to being taken over and not really running shit, to sort of exercising influence and then maybe inadequately running shit. That's just a little history lesson. One thing that has not changed, at least since I've been alive, is the wedding ritual.

First, there's the lamb sacrifice. I know this sounds barbaric, but it's supposed to bring years of luck to the bride and groom, *and* they've really modernized the whole process. See, after slitting the lamb's jugular vein, a national nonprofit that deals with the ritual sacrifice of lambs, which I believe is called The National Nonprofit that Deals with the Ritual Sacrifice of Lambs, is sent in to clean up any errant blood, collect the lamb, and distribute meaty lamb portions to families in need around the area.

Then the ceremony. The bride and groom sit under a

lacey thing as an elder—usually some kind of scholar—makes wise remarks about marriage. The elder ladies of both families rub blocks of sugar over the heads of the bride and groom representing eternal sweetness in the marriage. The *I do*s follow a hilarious patter. The bride is asked if she is willing to marry the groom and she sits there silently while the elder ladies chant something like "The bride is out picking flowers." The bride is asked again if she'll marry the groom, and again she sits in silence. Then more chanting from the ladies: "The bride is out at the market." This happens a few more times, just to keep the groom in a state of fake panic until finally she accepts. It's the kind of call-and-response ceremony that would make a Baptist church blush.

After the ceremony comes the reception. Everyone is dressed to the nines. Colognes and perfumes are intermingling in a dangerous potpourri of smells. And before the food even comes out, the Iranians are dancing. Grannies are dancing, little kids are dancing, the groom's childhood dentist is dancing, these people can't stop dancing. You know the stuffy weddings with the seating chart and the designated time for speeches and gentle waltzes? This is nothing like that. These people are in an eternal do-si-do of their own making. The bride and groom are in the middle of the room, hands in the air like they're at the top of a roller coaster (and like they don't care), squealing with delight and just a touch of uncertainty because this is the beginning and who knows what will come next?

The wedding formed the climax of this trip to Iran.

This was my first adult trip where I saw and understood the cycle of life as my family had lived it. I had carried so much guilt on this trip. The exchange rate made everything so cheap for my American dollar and I felt guilt. Putting on the hijab was such a funny novelty for me, but I knew I would go back to wearing my regular clothes, and I felt guilt. The ability to travel—generally without visas and suspicion—came so easily to me, and I felt guilt. I couldn't fathom the idea that my family lived full and happy lives. How could people feel happy without iPods and easily accessible beer? How could they be fulfilled without regime change?

True, people in Iran are waiting for regime change. But while my cousin waited for regime change she had found Mr. Right, she became an architect, found career success, and had a child. And I carried a guilt that seemed only to condescend to her. As an American, I sit at home, watch the news, and make a series of assumptions about other countries. But news stories don't form the picture. They only give us license to feel some kind of political and economic superiority. And I did. On this trip, at this most joyous of weddings, I found that it's a dangerous superiority that swallows the three-dimensionality of their lives. That my guilt is useless and belittling. That the Americanness of my opinions mattered not more, but just as much as anyone else's. The outlines of a responsibility began to take hold: I have to talk about them like they're people, not news stories.

CHAPTER 8

Where My Staplers At?

Spoiler alert: I graduated from college. I wore a skirt that was too short under my graduation gown and fully took advantage of the last time I could make out with a collegiate stranger. (Except for the time that I went back to college three years later for a sketch comedy group reunion, but that doesn't really count because I think he was more into the eighty-year-old British tea-time character I had been playing and not the *real* me.) I left Cornell and immediately went to Paris, where I thought my charms would land me very important work. Allow me to condense that experience into an easily digestible bullet point montage.

The Classic Postcollegiate European Experience Told in Montage

☐ I moved in with my friend Charmaine and pranced around Paris trying to emanate a certain, I don't know what, let's call it je ne sais quoi.

☐ I was hired to be a tourist shop trinket salesman at Montmartre, the hilltop home of the Sacré-Coeur—the kind of romantic destination where you could picture Pepe Le Pew hitting on you.

☐ I was apparently a terrible trinket salesman, so I was fired. Well, it was a probationary period so I like to think, We just weren't a good fit for each other, or rather, *On n'ira pas ensemble.*

☐ I then got a job teaching English to a bunch of businessmen (and one businesswoman). I was apparently the toast of the English center, because my California accent was in high demand. This was the only time that my accent has ever been a professional asset.

☐ I made out with a bunch of French dudes, including one who had Tourette's syndrome. In French, even Tourette's comes off as *ooh-la-la.*

☐ Charmaine and I always bought cheap wine that we put in the freezer so it was tolerable enough to drink. This invention became known as "the French Wine slushy." We would not go on to profit from this remarkable creation; however, it got us tanked on the cheap.

☐ We learned how to speak French le pretty fucking well.[1]

1. French translation: *On parlais francais dans un facon putain du merde de merveilleuse, tu vois? Par example, on a dit, "Nik ta mere, t'es fous toi!" parce que on a parlais si bien le francais.**

☐ I got myself a little French pseudoboyfriend. Charmaine got his best friend as a French pseudoboyfriend. ·
Keep it in *la famille*, as they say.

☐ I got into a bar fight with a nutjob[2] who thought my
boyfriend was stealing her beer. She hit me in the head
with a bottle while I stood there. She then climbed on
a stool to hit me again. I learned that when confronted
with violence, I totally do nothing and just get beat up. I
got stitches. But they were French stitches, so they were
very chic.

☐ I learned that the French have their own intense
racial hierarchies that revolve around their former colonial relationships with North and West African countries.
I also learned that racism and bigotry flourish in countries other than the United States. *Viva la France!*

☐ My work visa ran out and I went to London, where
I thought my co-English speakers would immediately hire
me to do something very important.

☐ I ended up waitressing. Was I at a really cute and
totally British pub? No. Was I at a really cute and totally
British shoppe? No. I was waiting tables at a Pizza Hut
near Victoria Station.

---

* English Translation: We spoke French really prostitute of shitting amazingly, you know? For example, we'd say, "Go fuck your mom, you fool!"
because that's how well we spoke French.
2. French Translation: *noisette* job.

☐ I learned that the British order shrimp on pizza, like psychopaths.

☐ I made out with four dudes named Simon. Four.

☐ I learned that the British drink too much.

☐ I gained fifteen pounds. But in Britain they weigh themselves in "stones," and fifteen pounds is only about one stone. So when you put it that way, it's almost like I lost weight.

☐ My closest friends in London—Julie and Florence—were French. I ended up speaking even better French, in London.

☐ I discovered that the roommates I found in the English equivalent of Craigslist were heroin addicts. As a sort of, by the book American, this freaked me out.

☐ I got fed up with the shrimp pizza and heroin-addicted roommates, so I went back to the United States to live with my parents for two months.

☐ Before I left my roommates, I angrily emptied their shampoo bottles to teach them a lesson about doing drugs. I then felt guilty and left my own shampoo behind as a backup. Why should a heroin addict's hygiene suffer? You can be strung out but still smell good.

☐ I worked at a DVD rental store that one of my best friends, Jennie, was managing. She admitted years later that I was a terrible employee. She also admitted it *while* I was a terrible employee.

☐ I moved to New York City.

Finding a job in New York City is a lot like walking through the desert without shoes on, listening to only the audio track of the movie *Gigli* on your earbuds, except your earbuds have a mild acid on them that is slowly burning your ear skin, and you see a mirage in the distance that would have kept you going if it wasn't for the fact that the mirage is Donald Trump and he's giving a speech on foreign policy. That's what an NYC job hunt is like: rather unpleasant.

I had a brief stint as a curatorial assistant for a historical collection of Revolutionary, early national, antebellum, and Civil War–era ephemera. What is Civil War ephemera? It's anything from a note that a gentleman wrote to a bureaucrat, or a note that a farmer wrote to a gentleman, or a note that a military man wrote another military man, or on very rare occasions a note that a farmer wrote to a military man. On even rarer occasions, it would be a note that a woman would write to a farmer to whom she was betrothed. (*Betrothed* was slang for "engaged" back then.) Mostly these notes would read like this:

Dear Sir,

Upon the Ordinance of the Fifth established parish of the Fourth county line within the Third Lunar passing of the Spring Equinox please be forewarned and please generally note in a form other than a warning that the meaZurements of this Parcel of Land have been calkulated upon the aforementioned Boundaries and have ThereFore been totaled at the very sum of 3 hectares by 4 hectares. The easement is recognized as One-Half of a cattle's width.

Yours truly in land speculation,
Sir Howard Beauregard Braintree

If you were riveted by this note, if you have found yourself saying, "Don't stop there, I want to hear more about the length and width of this parcel of land," then you would have been really jealous of me! Because I got to read ephemera like that *all day long.*

What does a historical collection need on an average day? It needs blurbs! Lots of blurbs! So I would look at a note from a general to, let's say, another general, during a skirmish, battle, or clash (all very different), and I would do a little historical research around the note. Not to brag, but the research involved one to two steps beyond Wikipedia. Then I would write a blurb! I wrote some great fucking blurbs up in that historical collection. My blurbs would make you feel anything ranging from begrudgingly interested to remarkably indifferent.

When I think back to this office, the words "children of the corn" come to mind. The people who helmed this collection were...a collection unto themselves. On my first day there, the boss walked in with a big box of donuts. I thought, How nice, he's bringing donuts for everyone on my first day. But he held on to that box, marched right into his office, and polished off those two dozen donuts, by himself.

And he was skinny. On my first meeting in his office, I saw candy everywhere. M&M's on bookshelves, Skittles in desk filing cabinets. The man had the organs of a Butterfinger.

At some point he noticed that I always reheated my coffee in the morning—I'm just one of those people who likes hot coffee, go figure. One day, I got up for my midmorning coffee reheat when I was startled by a stuffed bunny casually sitting in the microwave. The boss popped out laughing hysterically. "I punked you!" he said. This kind of thing happened all the time—trust me, *The Office* is real.

So I decided to blow that joint and explore other options, the kind of options that would let me pay my rent and my cell phone bill at the same time, in the same month. So I got a corporate job as an economic crime analyst. I was just like Edward Snowden, working on government projects contracted out to our private firm. Except I had no access to any sensitive data, and I totally didn't have high-level hacking skills or an interest in defecting to Russia. Otherwise, just like Edward Snowden.

My job was to investigate economic crimes, so when a huge company or a government lost a bunch of money in some major fraud situation, we would figure out how it happened. What I learned is companies that already make a lot of money get really mad when a comparatively small amount of money is stolen from them. Even if they're still on top of the world and still making a ton of money. Basically, it was like working for an aid organization, except the aid was doled out by one percenters for one percenters. And the aid workers in this case got nice, boozy lunches.

This was my first exposure to the moneyed class—

WHERE MY STAPLERS AT?   127

to people who understood what a "benchmark index" was and didn't care who knew it. I learned a lot about these people in the time I was a fake corporate drone:

RULES THAT ONE PERCENTER OFFICE BROS LIVE BY

- ☐ Gym is for lunch hour.
- ☐ Happy hour is for lunch.
- ☐ Steak consumption is a sign of power.
- ☐ If you don't have season tickets to high-profile sporting events, you're no better than an animal.
- ☐ Always take a crazy photo on a golf cart whenever you go on vacation.
- ☐ Always take a wacky photo on top of a ski slope.
- ☐ All packages should be delivered to the office, including the family pack of condoms from Amazon.
- ☐ Heaven doesn't accept people who stay at three-star hotels.
- ☐ The subway is full of savage plebeians except for you. You are an elegant, classy rider.
- ☐ Fantasy football should be scheduled into the workday.
- ☐ Stay at the office longer than your boss.
- ☐ Always get a car service after 8 P.M., even if your apartment is only five blocks away.
- ☐ Always get a car service before 8 A.M., even if your apartment is only five blocks away.

If I harbored any lingering doubts about whether I could be a part of Club White, this corporate job cleared it up for me. When the firm decided to ease the dress code, every white boy in the office came by my desk asking me not to fuck it up for everyone. I was doing comedy gigs at night, which gave me the reputation of a rabble-rouser, that is, investigator by day, comedian by night, and always donning "fun" outfits on Fridays. Everyone was concerned I would take my fun outfits too far. They wanted control of the fun outfits. They wanted a Stepford coworker— sister to the Stepford wife, except that she has a job and earns a living, but like the Stepford wife, she gets in line, doesn't say shit, and does *not* wear fun outfits.

It's no wonder that corporate offices attract sameness. Apparently "cultural fit" is the top hiring priority. Cultural fit doesn't ask, "Can an applicant do the job?" but "Do I want to hang out with this applicant?" To test cultural fit, a study out of Northwestern University found that bosses like to chat, they like to test personal chemistry by figuring out what a candidate is into:

> Bonding over rowing college crew, getting certified in scuba, sipping single-malt Scotches in the Highlands or dining at Michelin-starred restaurants was evidence of fit; sharing a love of teamwork or a passion for pleasing clients was not.[3]

So did I really have Stepford coworkers? Yes, yes I did. I had them by design. A design that stifles corporate

---

3. This is *Sunday New York Times* evidence, which means it came before an article about real estate and after an article about new uses for cumquats. See Lauren A. Rivera, "Guess Who Doesn't Fit In at Work," *New York Times*, May 30, 2015, http://www.nytimes.com/2015/05/31/opinion/sunday/guess-who-doesnt-fit-in-at-work.html?_r=0.

offices all over the country. We often blame the lack of diversity in the workplace on the job seekers—they don't try hard enough, they simply don't apply for these jobs. Or we somehow put the blame more abstractly on society. But the hiring process is very clearly managed by people. There's nothing abstract there. Even if minority candidates apply for a job and all their qualities are spot on, they still might not get the job, because "cultural fit" means sameness, it means comfort. And being around black, Latino, or uncategorizably ethnic people might not elicit comfort.

I get it. It's easier to work with people who are like you. And if you're a minority, I hate to add another item to your endless to-do list, but this is where you disarm them with something other than a shared collegiate sports team. (This is where you make...white people laugh. *Oh she said the name of the book in the book again! AH!*) And I'm not saying to be an Uncle Tom—or an Uncle Karime or an Aunt Katsumi—you don't have to pretend to embrace all of their whiteness. You're not in a polo club, and that's *fine*. But open the door and don't be forgettable.

I like to make myself the butt of the joke. I ask questions and riff! "Oh, you like to ski? I went on a bunny slope once, and ended up with a broken pinky toe." "Oh, you're from Nebraska? I once got hit with a batch of poison ivy right outside Johnny Carson's childhood home in Nebraska." "Oh, you like hockey? I don't go to hockey games because I have an irrational fear of the puck hitting me in the face."

I find the *in* and make the connection. Even if they have more money and power than you, even if they have seen the world and have an investment portfolio, even if they show up to work on a gold-plated scooter, they will respond to someone with a light heart who treats them as an equal. Talk to them like you're talking to your idiot best friend from middle school—only with bits of professionalism on the edges.

White people, you're not off the hook. Step out of your comfort zone, because you may end up with a better workforce. But you don't even have to listen to me! Listen to researcher Katherine Phillips: She found in a study that "diverse groups outperformed more homogeneous groups not because of an influx of new ideas, but because diversity triggered more careful information processing that is absent in homogeneous groups."[4] *BAM!* You'll make more money. Don't you want to make more money?

Once you're there, you should learn the lay of the land, because offices are a political minefield. The good news is that because we have bred this sameness for many generations, you'll find a reliable set of categorizable people, delineated in the graph on the next page.

In my office dealings, I also learned to stay away from very sexual interns. I learned that unkempt IT dudes were also most likely to store photos from my laptop in a personal stash. I learned that whenever I have a document to fill out that I don't understand, I should bypass all

---

4. "Better Decisions Through Diversity," *Kellogg Insight* (blog), October 1, 2010, Northwestern University, Kellogg School of Management, http://insight .kellogg.northwestern.edu/article/better_decisions_through_diversity.

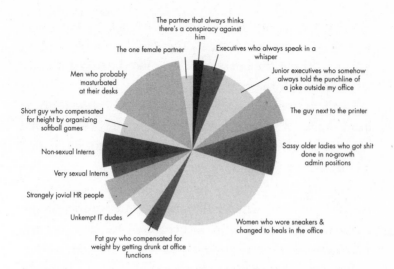

The partner that always thinks there's a conspiracy against him

The one female partner

Men who probably masturbated at their desks

Short guy who compensated for height by organizing softball games

Non-sexual Interns

Very sexual Interns

Strangely jovial HR people

Unkempt IT dudes

Fat guy who compensated for weight by getting drunk at office functions

Executives who always speak in a whisper

Junior executives who somehow always told the punchline of a joke outside my office

The guy next to the printer

Sassy older ladies who got shit done in no-growth admin positions

Women who wore sneakers & changed to heals in the office

Negin's Corporate Office Population Breakdown

the junior executives and head straight to the sassy older ladies who get shit done, because they'll actually be able to help me. I also learned that I was missing out on huge promotion potential, because I didn't go to basketball games and my parents didn't have a weekend home in Sag Harbor where I could invite everyone on a summer Friday. I could hold down a drink, but otherwise, the social engagement that got my coworkers their promotions and bonuses and pats on the back was very white and very masculine.

In fact, at the end of my first year there I learned that I had been hired at $5,000 less a year than my male counterparts. That's right—someone let it slip that the two women in my cohort were paid less than the men. The only nice thing I can say about this is that sexism is reliable. It will always hurt. And when a corporation can save a buck by exercising it, they will. Reliably. I guess it's nice taking the guesswork out, like I know I'll make less because of the tits! Wee!

In the same way that office sameness wasn't in my head, unequal pay isn't in my head, either. The national statistic cited by the White House still points out that women earn 78 cents for every dollar a man earns.[5] Even if you break it down by field, lawyer ladies, physician broads, and CEO chicks all earned less than their counterparts with testicles (78.8 percent, 71.7 percent, and 79.9 percent respectively).[6] So, no one is making it up.

What was worse was that when I found out I was paid less, I did absolutely nothing with that information. I didn't want to seem disagreeable. I wanted to keep my job because I needed it. I got scared. Like a dumbass. If more women talk about their pay, more women will eventually realize they're not getting equal pay. And then maybe they can do something about it. Unlike me.

Speaking of cash monies, this job was also the first time I learned about bonus season. Come January every year, the people of the wide-ranging financial arts are given really nice little gifts from their jobs. I know what

5. "Your Right to Equal Pay: Did You Know That Women Are Still Paid Less Than Men?" White House, https://www.whitehouse.gov/equal-pay/career.
6. Sarah Hedgecock, "Report: Most Men Still Out-Earn Most Women," *Gawker*, May 28, 2014, http://gawker.com/report-most-men-still-out -earn-most-women-1582628892.

you're thinking: It's nice for an employer to give a bonus. When I got that $25 gift certificate at Starbucks from my boss, I felt pretty good about it. But bonuses here were more like Starbucks gift cards times five thousand. I never forgot the grabby-handedness of the office bros during bonus season.

Little did I know that a few years later, when I was entrenched in the world of social justice comedy, those bonuses would come back and tickle me in the armpits, and I would turn around and slap them. In other words, issues around banking and finance became a big part of my work. In fact, years later I would crush hard on financial issues. They are *soooo borring* and yet *soooo important*. The way *your* money is handled and the way the money from people with far more resources is handled are worlds apart. The average person doesn't have a team that can figure out how to legally bypass various taxes. But one percenters do. They have teams! Teams that probably wear ties and/or respectable but sporty slacks on more casual workdays!

In 2008, if you'll recall, the government spent billions of dollars to bail out a bunch of banks.[7] This has generated an ongoing tax subsidy to the too-big-to-fail banks to the tune of $83 billion a year.[8] Every year. You'd think that in light of that bailout, they would tighten the ol'

---

7. We fronted $700 billion on the bailout, but figures on what it ultimately cost the taxpayer vary from $24 billion to $80 billion.
8. "Remember That $83 Million Bank Subsidy? We Weren't Kidding," *Bloomberg View* February 24, 2013, http://www.bloombergview.com /articles/2013-02-24/remember-that-83-billion-bank-subsidy-we-weren't -kidding.

purse strings, or pull in the ol' belt loop, or double-knot the ol' sneakers. I'm sure there were some purse-, belt-, and sneaker-related modifications to their internal workings. But one practice that remained, in full force, were their annual bonuses.

In the year 2013, bankers received over $91 billion in bonuses.[9] We did some crude math and figured that this averaged out to about $300,000 per person. These aren't people that are earning shitcakes the rest of the year. They're high earners, so $300,000 is just an added benefit, or what is popularly referred to as a bonus—a term you have seen me use. The bonuses seemed to be a bit much, especially considering that the bailout was for $83 billion, an amount that was loaned with no interest and hasn't been fully repaid.

Armed with this information, I partnered with the Other 98% and took to the streets! The Other 98% is a nonprofit organization and a grassroots network of concerned people that shines a light on economic injustice, undue corporate influence, and threats to democracy. They named themselves before "1 percent" became the outcry of a nation. With a cameraman in tow, I asked regular people about banking bonuses and little-known fact: Most people don't know about banking bonuses. Making banking bonuses themselves a little-known fact.

But the pièce de résistance was a petition, signed by

---

9. "The Other 98% Urges Wall Street to Donate $91 Billion in Bonuses to Victims of Financial Crisis," *Democracy Now!* December 27, 2013, http://www .democracynow.org/2013/12/27/occupy_offshoot_urges_wall_street_to.

over thirty thousand people, directed at Bank of America, asking the CEO for a change. Instead of doling out bonuses to already financially well-off bankers, why not turn that money over to create housing for the 10 million people who were made homeless...by the housing crises...the housing crisis that was created from the financial meltdown...that was created from the banks... the banks that needed bailing out...from the government...funded by the taxpayers.

Look, I don't have a problem with people being rich. I just don't understand why they have to be so so so rich while everyone else has to pay a higher rate of taxation on their meager incomes—and then watch those taxes get redirected to bailouts. It seems, you know, unfair, like how can skinny people like the freak boss at my first job eat a million donuts all day and never get fat? (On an unrelated note, fuck those skinny people.)

I took this petition to the Bank of America headquarters and attempted to meet with the president of the bank. To my great surprise, chagrin, and dismay he wouldn't see me. Yes, I'm sure you're all surprised that the president of a major U.S. bank with assets of over $2.10 trillion[10] wouldn't meet an Iranian-American Muslim Social Justice Comedian in an imposing red lipstick towering over everyone at five foot three-point-five inches whose other main task for the day was refining a bit about "running into her trainer at a pastry shop." Not to worry—I was

---

10. "Bank of America Total Assets (Quarterly)," YCharts, http://ycharts.com/companies/BAC/assets.

assured by the "security desk" that my petition would make it to his office.

I'd like to live in a world where it did. As every social justice comedian knows, you have to operate from a place where you think that petition actually made it to the CEO of Bank of America. And that one day, there will be a CEO who has an epiphany, an epiphany brought on by your petition. Or a flaming bag of dog shit you left in front of their mansion. Whichever. Okay, don't leave a flaming bag of dog shit—I found out the hard way that it's alienating.

When Sunbathing Meets Offshore Banking

The other thing corporate America taught me is the extent to which people want *not* to pay taxes. Oh, the lengths the moneyed people will go to avoid paying for the taxes that pay for stuff like roads and schools; oh, what fun they have figuring out new and creative ways of hiding their money.

In 2012 I went to the Cayman Islands with fellow comedian Lee Camp and Eric, our terrific DP (in this case DP stands for "director of photography," not the more common "double penetration"), and a brave coproducer, Justin. We were funded in part by the Other 98% and the Yes Men—the Yes Men is an organization known for its sneaky ways in publicly shaming, laughing at, or simply uncovering the truth of all manner of social ills.

The Cayman Islands is known as an offshore banking

haven. It's the kind of tax haven that gives its banking clients an opportunity to get a really nice tan after they've spent an exhausting hour moving funds from one bank to another bank, or worse yet, from a briefcase to a bank. Offshore banking also requires readily accessible wind-sailing and spas. Don't underestimate how much goes into making a world-renowned tax haven.

To explain offshore tax havens a bit, you know how you could be a barista / schoolteacher / IT guy for fifty hours a week, and right after you disinfect your foot blisters / redline homework assignments / massage your carpel tunnel, you look at your paystub and notice how much you paid in taxes? Tax haven-ites don't know what that's like.

They hide that money, and the federal government loses something like $150 billion in tax revenue, mostly from people who have a special relationship with yachts and/or seasonal residences and/or calming bath salts.[11] Of course, $150 billion is just an estimate, because we don't know how much money is being hidden. Because it's hidden.

The thing about hiding money, too, is that the people who are making the money, they still take advantage of stuff like roads, trash collection, running water, and sewage—so when they're taking sweet dumps in their toilets, dumps that are then taken away by city sewage and water systems, they're not paying the taxes that make those sweet dumps possible. Basically, what they should

---

11. "Report: Close Corporate Tax Loopholes," U.S. PIRG, http://www .uspirg.org/reports/usp/hidden-cost-offshore-tax-havens.

be doing is (1) holding it in, or (2) paying taxes. But with offshore tax havens, they get to do both.

So I went to the Cayman Islands in 2012 right before the presidential elections. Our goals were to (a) look for Mitt Romney's money and (b) open an offshore bank account. At the time, Mitt Romney was a presidential nominee with an estimated net worth of $250 million—that made him one of the richest presidential candidates in the history of candidates. Sorry, Warren G. Harding, I guess being a newspaper editor just isn't as lucrative, especially if our metric is "boat ownership." But questions arose about where and how that money was being made. In some tax returns he listed Swiss bank accounts, in others he didn't. He also set up shell corporations in the Cayman Islands that he argued were legal—shell companies are like inactive zombie companies used to move money around. But, when it comes to Cayman tax havens, asking for information is banned—there's a confidentiality law stipulating that even asking about financial disclosures could get you jailed for up to four years. That tax haven don't fuck around.

So Lee and I went on a mission to find Romney's money. The island is full of sand and sport, beautiful blue waters, and a collection of "business" buildings. One such building is Ugland House. Ugland has nineteen thousand businesses registered to it. I'm not sure what any of these businesses did, because Ugland was a small five-story building. It didn't seem to have a stream of workers coming in and out, taking cigarette breaks after a long morning of making widgets. If you divided the square footage of the buildings by the number of business registered to it, each business would be three to four square inches big. Our guess was that each building provided an address for an endless number of shell corporations that housed endless millions. After asking locals and administrators about where we could find Romney's "corporation," we realized that the Caymanians were serious about zipping their lips. But we suspected the money was kept at the Ugland House.

If Romney could keep untaxed money at the Ugland House, that was clearly where we should put *our* money! Not to brag, but at that point, after every month's bills were paid off, I had a cool $5–$25 in disposable income weighing me down; Lee had the same. So, we walked into Ugland and proudly asked if we could open up an offshore bank account with our disposable income of $8.46. We were told to stop filming. We kept filming from a—no joke—camera pen on Lee's lapel. They called security. We left, tried another bank. They called security. We tried another bank. They called security. By the end of the third security call, we were very nervous that we would be jailed for up to four years because we asked questions. We were worried about being kicked out of the country, or kept in the country against our will, or forced to go tanning with Mitt Romney. These fears were probably unfounded, but when you're in the thick of it, when there's a security guard blaring at you, it's hard to distinguish. Either way, we took the footage home and cut together a video, then put it online.

The offshore tax havens in the Cayman Islands solidified what I learned at that first corporate job. I was exposed not only to the sameness that rankles the corporate world but to the lengths people and companies will go to earn more money. After a little over a year at that job, having used the printer and laminator for every imaginable task,[12] I decided it was time to go to grad school. If anything, being around corporate folk—with their expense accounts, extra pairs of shoes under their desks, tape dispensers, and casual cultural bias—being around them made me feel even more of an outsider, made me feel more committed to the black cause. Of course, I hadn't figured out yet that I actually might have my own cause.

Corporate America also made me feel more committed to public service. I didn't want to expend my energy helping Fortune 500s find lost money. I wanted to help people with no money have the opportunity of ever getting money at all. Or justice. Or just...something nice out of life. So that was when I applied to the African-American Studies program at Columbia University. (Please reread the Introduction for an incomplete but hopefully entertaining account of that time.)

But being around these corporate dudes with their concentrated wealth and money also made me realize how much I wanted to bring them into the fold. How, ultimately, they're a part of the solution. How they're not bad people, they just don't *see* what the problem is. Why would they? They're surrounded by comfort and really great laminators. So we have to figure out how to bring them into the fold.

---

12. What? Don't act like you haven't dreamed of having access to a laminator. Don't act like you haven't looked at a grocery list and thought, What this grocery list needs is to be laminated.

CHAPTER 9

My Own People Don't Like
Me Very Much

As I mentioned before, Muslims don't necessarily have the greatest icons here in the United States. The ones we do have are on the crap spectrum—that's the end of the spectrum that's loaded with bigotry, essentializing, infantilizing, theologocentrism,[1] and dog poop. Oh yes, I did just casually use the word *theologocentrism* like it was no big deal. Dropping ten-dollar words has the subtextual weight of saying, *"I read a book once."*

Pretentious ten-dollarness aside, here's the deal with theologocentrism: Scholars have had a tendency to explain all observable phenomenon in a majority Muslim country by saying, basically, "they're like that because of Islam."

---

1. *Europe and the Mystique of Islam* by Maxime Rodinson and Roger Veinus—also discussed here: Rachel Woodlock, "Angels or Animals? The Problem of Muslim Stereotyping," *Religion and Ethics*, ABC, April 3, 2012, http://www.abc.net.au/religion/articles/2012/04/03/3469636.htm.

In some major corners of academia, Islam is a catchall for anything a researcher doesn't understand. Of course it's not limited to academia. The world of infotainment has also grabbed hold of Islam to explain things they can't fully comprehend, by which I mean everything. It's easier to say, "Post-9/11 terrorism exists because of Islam" than it is to say, "Post-9/11 terrorism exists because the western response to that act of terrorism has been addled by inconsistent policy processes that focused more on war than on nation building, and those shortcomings have in turn created an environment in which antiwestern sentiment might thrive."[2] See! That shit can't fit on a poster, much less in Don Lemon's mouth.

Because everything spins on Islam's wheels, it's easy to fall into the trap where we take the icons we're given—like gun-toting terrorists or burka-clad ladies—and fight them on their own merits. We end up saying stuff like, "You can't say that Muslims are terrorists because Islam is *peaceful*!" I've personally gone on rants trying to explain to people: "Hold up! Muslims exists on a spectrum; some are very conservative, and others are as secular as your best Christian friend who only goes to church once a year and/or never but still call themselves Christian. What's the diff, guys!?"

We twist ourselves into knots convincing people that Islam is peaceful and varied before we realize that, wait a second, you can be a Muslim while also recognizing that

---

2. You want to know who's badass on this issue? David Rothkopf and his book *National Insecurity*. I wasn't quoting him, but I do kinda wish he one day reads this book and blesses my quote with some kind of elaborate Rothkopfian seal.

Islam doesn't even explain half of your behaviors! Islam can be peaceful all it wants. It's not the only relevant detail about a group of people. *Islam* is a hot-button word in the United States, but what if it doesn't explain anything about us? What if it doesn't explain terrorism at all?

It's not in the scope of this book for me to explain terrorism—there's plenty of smart people to do that who are not comedians by trade. But I mention it because the need to shoehorn Islam as the major reason for everything in post-9/11 America defines so much of how we see mainstream American Muslims. We've created an arsenal of icons based on this shoehorning, and those icons do not represent me or fit my worldview.

Okay, so if you're like me, you might think there must be cultural touchstones from the mother country to hold on to. Iranians certainly don't define *themselves* as Islamic terrorists. But there again, for the hyphenated types—your Iranian-Americans, your Moroccan-Irish-Americans—the traditional icons from the mother country don't always work, either. For example, Iranians love poetry. That's a nice stereotype and there's truth to it because when in doubt, Iranians will bust out some totally insightful Rūmī poem in Farsi. Somehow reciting poetry settles questions, quiets arguments—it's like eating mac 'n' cheese, it makes Iranians feel all warm and mushy inside. But being a poetry nerd doesn't really speak to *me*. I don't know any of Rūmī's poems. No offense—I'm sure he was a nice guy—but I'm American, so his oeuvre is alien to me. I'm more likely to recite Mos Def. And if you're Russian-American, you don't want wooden dolls inside of slightly bigger wooden dolls inside of slightly bigger wooden dolls. You take gin instead of vodka, you might prefer BLTs to borsht and you kinda don't "get" Yakov Smirnoff.

But at the same time you might not understand why Americans go Dutch on bills,[3] why they're so friendly to strangers, or why they take improv classes. Because you're not fully American, either, you're this Third Thing, you're a *Russian-American* and you have to forge this Third Thing identity in the United States. And it's not easy.

Like the hypothetical Russian-American, I'm a Third Thing—Islam doesn't explain me, Iranian poetry doesn't explain me, and apple pie doesn't explain me. And yet I understand all of those things. Being a Third Thing is a designation for people who straddle worlds, who may have a foot in every door yet their butt is hovering between door frames and they may even have more than two feet, and either way they're definitely going to pull a groin muscle.

How do you know you're a Third Thing? For me, after the world got stuffed with Muslim iconography I didn't recognize but was lumped into, that was when I knew. You know because you've been squeezed into a category that may technically be true but still doesn't fit right. You squirm in it. It's like having a rock in your shoe or wearing underwear that rides up your junk. Sure, they're technically underpants, but they don't fit right. Sure, I'm Muslim, but the way some people say it rides up my junk.

---

3. By the way, do Dutch people even do this??

You also know you're a Third Thing when you hang out with friends and you will totally dump on your own people but get *very mad* when anyone else tries to join in on the dumping. I can say all I want about Iran, but *you!?* You better be careful, because I'm not gonna let no one talk shit about Iran! *But, you were just saying how*—nuh-uh, zip it! You're a Third Thing when you *complain* about the identity and you *defend* the identity in equal parts.

I know a fair number of black Americans—some of my best friends are black.[4] Some are of Caribbean or West Indian descent. They have to fly the Third Thing hard. I had a friend who would constantly correct people—"I'm not African-American, I'm from Trinidad"—but when black people were under attack, he would immediately switch to "As a black American" and drop the Trinidad. It never seemed odd to me. He just didn't want to be lumped into the black American population. He didn't want people to wholesale erase Trinidad. Why do people feel the need to erase anything? Let the man be a Third Thing!

If you're not a Third Thing, let me try to explain the *feeling*. Have you ever been at a summer camp that was overly athletic? (...she says, having been at a summer camp that was overly athletic.) You're supposed to be excited, you're supposed to have fun, your parents drop you off at this day camp every morning and you are filled with...dread. And then one day you find out that some

---

4. It's funny, because some people say that to defend horrible shit.

of the kids are doing crafts off the field in a room, with window screens to keep out the bugs, and you ask if you can join them and be a part of that summer camp? There's papier-mâché and paints and puppets, and it is heavenly. That's when you know, you are the kind of person who likes "summer camp" writ large, but you're not the type of person that likes the sports part. Some might call you a nerd. If sports and arts and summer camp were nations, immigration stories and ethnicities, you would be a Third Thing. Except that Third Things are kind of third-y all their lives, and summer camp is only six weeks long.

Even though my parents are full-on Iranians, I never learned the intricate customs—there's a far-reaching set of rules and a whole language of etiquette. It's so complicated! You could offer to buy someone a coffee and it could be interpreted as an insult depending on the other person's relative age, income, citizenship status, gender, level of indigestion...I mean, it's *nuts*. My parents gave me some basic Iranian rules but by no means all of them (plus I think they find it hilarious when they see me struggle). So, when I meet Iranians, I can speak to them in Farsi, and I can say nonformal American-style greetings, but I'm always inadvertently breaking rules that I didn't even know existed!

All of this happens because I'm that weird Third Thing and I'm trying to forge my own way, but it's not easy. And when you're a Third Thing, you're addressing a heretofore nonexistent Third Thing Audience or Third Thing Sympathizing Audience. You're now the de facto voice of your people's Third Thing subgroup, and the people in the First and Second Things aren't necessarily going to like it.

This could mean many things

I feel like I've been trying to build a Third Thing Sympathizing Audience since I was a kid. In the professional world of comedy, trying to forge this Third Thing identity has been a *task*, lemme tell ya! I mentioned this project before but, I made a film for which me and fellow comedian Dean Obeidallah rounded up a bunch of Muslim-American comedians—in a nonviolent way—and we toured the country. We went to places like Tennessee, Alabama, Mississippi, Georgia, Arizona, you know, places where they naturally love the

Muzzies. We called the tour (and subsequent film) *The Muslims Are Coming!* which to some meant "preventative warning lecture on the coming Muslim apocalypse" and to others meant "live Muslim fetish adult pornography." To most it meant "stand-up comedy show featuring Muslims."

We filmed the shows, which were free and open to the public, as long as the public was okay with the occasional swear word and with seeing an unusually brown lineup. We made the shows free because we wanted to remove all barriers to entry. If you were like "Eh, I'm not sure about those Muslims and besides, *I'm broke*," we didn't want the broke-ness to be an excuse. We didn't want you to choose between "Hot Pockets from the Piggly Wiggly for dinner" or "tickets to a comedy show featuring a bunch of Muz-types"—we wanted you to have the Hot Pocket *and* the Muz-types in one delicious, incongruent meal, high on carbs, high on fat, and well over your recommended daily dosage of Muslims.

Now I'm not gonna lie: When we first set out to do these shows, there was a lot of concern. Friends in New York thought that people in the deep South were going to react badly. They thought that people would say mean things and maybe even...do something physically violent. I definitely was not as concerned about the violence because I thought, come on, I look like a cartoon character, with the voice of Butters from *South Park*. How could anyone attack me?

And yet, we did plenty to elicit public attention. We would set up an "Ask a Muslim" booth in the middle of a town center so people could ask us questions. We invited people to come "Bowl with a Muslim"—an event that taught us

An actual photo of Negin reading a newspaper

that Muslims bowl very badly. (This explains why Barack Obama bowls so badly.[5]) We handed out flyers at farmers markets and gun shows and we were generally *visible*.

It was the visibility that had my friends and family concerned. Let's be honest—the South gets a pretty bad rap. They thought those Southerners were gonna brutalize me. That they were gonna unfurl large-scale Confederate flags and protest my shows. That they were going to show up

---

5. Again, Obama is not a Muslim; he was just accused of being a Muslim so that people wouldn't vote for him. It was an accusation that worked really well, because a majority of voters in some states continue to think he is a Muslim (Mississippi, I'm looking at you). (He did not win that state.) He is, however, a bad bowler, a quality he shares with Muslims. That, and an unwavering commitment to Allah. (*Kidding!* He's not Muslim.)

chewing tobacco and demanding the immediate deportation of all Muslim comedians.

Basically, the South has a PR problem not unlike that of Muslims. Because the Southerners I met (not to mention the large number of Mormons I met in Utah and Idaho) were far from that. They were open, welcoming. They had honest questions about us—questions like why don't we denounce terrorism, or would Goldfish constitute halal food. I didn't find them particularly racist, I didn't think they were trying to run me out of town, and I generally had a great time. I did see too much gun appreciation in the South, but nobody's perfect.

THE BEST, MOST HORRIBLE GUILTY PLEASURE SHOWS AND THE SOUTHERN STEREOTYPES THEY SHOWCASE

1. *Here Comes Honey Boo Boo*—If the South were judged on this show, then it's full of stage moms and/or people nick-named "Chubbs" and/or people who happily self-identify as rednecks and/or believers in the healing power of cheese puffs.
2. *Duck Dynasty*—If everyone in the South were like *Duck Dynasty* they would be proudly redneck (which is slightly different from "happily identifying as redneck"), zealous hunters, and all gun enthusiasts.
3. *Nashville*—This scripted hour-long drama teaches us that old money rules, Southerners still wear hats at certain horse-based events, and you should never trust anyone who's trying to launch a country music career.

Traveling in Arizona presented its own can of worms, or rather a can of lizards, because the climate there is too dry to support worms. We really wanted to film in Arizona because of SB 1070, a draconian law that allows cops to stop anyone if they suspect the (brown) person doesn't have papers. This is the kind of law that's secretly (but maybe overtly) designed to scare Mexicans, mostly the undocumented ones. It's a self-deportation law that's lousy on civil rights; what's worse, it could lead to bigoted action by law enforcement that's weirdly legal. It could just as easily be used to scare people in other brown groups, like Muslim ones, or really tan white people wearing turbans. Oh yeah, mark my words, turbans are the next fedora.

In fact, a good family friend was stopped in Arizona under the auspices of SB 1070. She's a nice, Iranian lady in her sixties, an American citizen, and has been living here for decades. She was driving her Mercedes through Flagstaff, looking at new houses because she was thinking of moving there. A cop stopped her because he thought she looked shifty. They asked to see her papers. That was when she launched into a lecture. She gave the cop a total talking-to in eloquent and perfectly threatening English on the nature of freedom, the beauty of civil rights, the ideological reasons that drew her to the United States. By the end, the cop was like "May I leave?" Turns out stopping a supposed illegal wasn't worth a lecture. She decided not to move to Arizona. The police there pose a very real threat. Even when you do have papers, being stopped at will does not make someone feel like they are a part of this great American experiment.

SB 1070 aside, it turns out that it was our own show in Tucson at the El Casino Ballroom that had me rattled. It was not a comedy club by any means, but the kind of cavernous hall where families might have quinceañeras, or maybe a local group could stage dance contests, or maybe the Hell's Angels could have a regional meetup, or...you get my point, there was some notable square footage. It was awesome and we sold out the four-hundred-person room to an extremely diverse crowd. Except "sold out" implies we sold tickets, which we didn't; that shit was free.

In most of the cities we traveled to, we performed to mostly white audiences. There weren't many Muslims in the audience at all, because (a) there aren't that many Muslims in the United States (varying estimates show that 1–4 percent of the population is Muslim), and (b) Muslims are presumably already on board with the message of the tour, so no need to beat a dead horse. But the Tucson audience was about 15 percent Muslim. We were surprised, because we just didn't know that Tucson had so many Muslims—let alone Muslims who like to go out and see comedy. I got on stage to do my set, peppered as it is with dating jokes, a riff on Truck Nutz, musings on the role of genitals in international diplomacy, and a couple of hilarious renditions of my mother in various states of disappointment.

During my set shit got, as they say in the industry, *real*. A group of Muslim women wearing the hijab were seated together (the hijab, you'll recall, is what Muz ladies cover their hair with and sometimes couple it with a long, jackety thing). There were maybe twenty of them. During the genital and dating stuff, one lady motioned for all the girls to get up and leave. They all did. It was quite a display, and they were very noticeable. I had to pretend like it wasn't happening, and the other 380 audience members had to pretend like they weren't distracted. After they left, I had to continue my set while pretending that I didn't want to hurl myself in front of a bus or—to be less morbid—in front of a slow-moving bicycle.

Those ladies walked out on me because they considered my material "shameful." To a regular American audience there's a lot of run-of-the-mill misogyny (women aren't funny, etc.). But the crudeness of the material is generally upheld as a gleaming example of the extent to which lewdness is welcomed in comedy. My material isn't racier than the average comic's, not by a long shot. But to that Muslim minority in the audience, it was shameful. The male comic before me did a bit on how he found a stack of porn mags as a teenager. It was a great bit and no one in the audience left. Is there a double standard? Maybe. It wouldn't be surprising to me if these Muslims felt that jokes were best served with a side of penis.

That isn't the only time this kind of thing happened to me. I learned after my first year of stand-up that I didn't quite have an obvious audience for my material. Some comedians have a clear audience; they can say, "Gay men love my act," or "Suburban moms really identify with my kid material," or "Broadway stagehands love my prop comedy." I didn't know who my audience was. I had been doing stand-up in New York to fun, generally progressive crowds. But then I had one of my first paying gigs out of town, in Chicago. I was so excited! I was getting paid, bitches! I was professionalizing! I arrived at Northwestern University in Chicago, marched onto the stage with pizzazz and a zest for life, and spoke for twenty solid minutes...to crickets.

What I didn't realize at the time was that this was an Iranian audience—no white person to be found. It was a mix of immigrants, like my parents, and college-aged Iranian students. The Middle Eastern student group that brought me out decided to invite Iranians in the larger community. Those Iranians were parents and uncles and general elders to the younger students. It seemed that because of their aunties' presence, the students didn't feel comfortable laughing at any of my dating material. Laughing would be tantamount to *admitting they've ever had sex*!

As audience members filed out, one woman told another woman, within earshot, that I was a whore. Everyone else left silently, avoiding eye contact. The producer of the show looked at me like I had killed a hamster.

So...that didn't go well. But it was only the beginning, because as my stand-up started popping up on YouTube I started getting comments like "Suck my proud Persian cock, you fucking whore" among other memorable zingers. Evidentially, the Internet isn't just for buying embarrassing products in bulk—like toilet paper and off-season supplies of Cadbury Mini Eggs—but it's also where people go to let off some bigoted and/or misogynistic steam.

I learned a lot about tailoring my material to different audiences, and I also learned not to read YouTube comments because they're generally *violent*, and it can't sit well with your soul. But I also learned that people like me have to break through, that we can't censor ourselves. Self-censoring doesn't help. I can't pretend like I don't date or that I've never had sex. Sure, I can avoid cursing—like I would on network television or when volunteering with young children—but I can't fundamentally deny my own life.

I've done comedy everywhere—the South, the Midwest, big cities, small towns—and I've performed for white audiences, mixed audiences, and Muslim audiences. I'm not saying I've never heard racist shit come out of white audiences (and I'll talk about that later). But I *am* saying that I've received some of the most heartbreaking resistance to my comedy from *my own people.*

You might think that your abuela is totally cool with your stance on gay rights or your farm-to-table cooking practices. You might think your Lebanese parents will understand your need to cross-dress or cross-stitch or whatever it is that helps you express your you-ness. You might think that your Muslim brothers and sisters *want* to hear you on that stage—that they will have your back—that they'll be the *last* people to walk out on you. But that might not be the case. Or it might be. People are complicated. But I do know you can't assume support just because you share a background. You're a Third Thing. It's different.

After every instance of my own people not liking me very much—the folks that call me a whore, the hate mail, the death threats, the walkouts—I pick myself up, dust myself off, and reapply some moisturizer. I use comedy to get through social interactions. I act like a tough mother-fucker. But inside I'm tore up. I feel like this Lego version of Optimus Prime, let's say, I have these huge, power-ful arms and they seem indestructible. Someone hurls an insult that dislodges my arm, and it just falls to the ground. Because those parts *are* destructible. They're just Legos. The pieces are still there, scattered on the ground and after one good cry, a strongly worded tweet, and a couple of bouts of self-doubt, I take those Legos and I start building that tough motherfucker up again. If I don't get back up, the Decepticons will win—and those guys are total dicks.

It just goes to show that it ain't easy being (a) green and (b) a Third Thing hyphenated American. So when you go out there to make white people laugh, don't expect your own people to follow you. It's possible they won't even like you very much. But that's okay, your stuff isn't *for them*. Forget comedy—when you strike out on your own to set your career in motion, to date, to sing kara-oke, to wear leggings, you can't assume that your friends and family will just be okay with it all. You'll launch an app, you'll write songs, you'll design logos, you'll draft buildings, and use algorithms, and there's no telling what you can do—and whatever route you take, you may have inexplicable opposition from your own people. But again, your life isn't for them. Let them come around.

CHAPTER 10

A Taxonomy of Haters

If you've never traveled the great expanse of the United States, you're missing out. As a comic, I've been to a lot of places. I've driven a lot of cars, and I've sat in and/ or napped in even more cars. I have seen multilane freeways, single-lane roadways, interstates, service roads, and off-ramps. I've driven on porous asphalt, reinforced concrete tarmac, and gravel. I've been fooled too many times by mini speed bumps—the kind that make you think you have a flat tire. Then you're like Oh no, I don't have a flat, I'm just on one of those roads with the mini speed bumps, what are those things called? Am I making up the term *mini speed bump*, or am I some kind of transportation expert whose command of freeway jargon comes naturally? These are the kinds of thoughts I'd have in, let's say, the roads of eastern Kentucky. Nice place, great walleye fishing.

Oh, and America, she is a beaut! Woody Guthrie was right—you'll see anything from the Redwood Forest to the Gulf Stream waters; you'll also see Waffle Houses, abandoned malls, office parks, and shooting ranges with a smattering of diabetes, anorexia, and credit card debt. Driving in the South is particularly fascinating, because you see swampland (and Waffle Houses). On the *Muslims Are Coming!* tour we saw a huge Confederate flag somewhere in Georgia billowing in the wind (near a Waffle House). We obviously needed to stop and add this to our photostream, because in Manhattan, it is not every day that you see a colossal Confederate flag set in a perfectly manicured field of grass. Talk about majesty. Though, actually, seeing that flag is rather commonplace for some parts of the South, not all parts. We stopped to roll the cameras. It was like taking a picture of racism, expressed in old-timey graphic design. That was when a gentleman came out to ask us what we were doing. He had the mien of someone who knew how to build a deck with his bare hands while reciting Faulkner. He inspired a certain kind of genteel masculine fear.

We exchanged the usual pleasantries that a band of comedians would exchange with the proprietor of a significant parcel of land showcasing a Confederate flag. We explained that we hadn't really seen a Confederate flag of such breadth before, and that we really wanted to get some footage of it. Now, when you're a bunch of brown comedians—with a film crew of two white dudes and a Latino guy—you may or may not stick out in the Deep South. We would regularly put Blair and Torey—the cinematographer and second camera operator—ahead of us to create a calming effect on passersby in these iffy situations. But here we were scattered among the errant livestock that grazed around the flag.

We expected some kind of "Get off my (supersized) lawn!" response, but the man was actually pleased that we were shooting footage. However, he wanted us to know one thing: "This isn't a Confederate flag, it's a flag from the collection of eleven states just after the Colonial era." Er, say what? You mean, the eleven states that comprised the *Confederacy*? Because what you're saying sounds like what we're saying, only not at all.

THE CONFEDERATE FLAG AND GEORGIA

This was Georgia's state flag from 1956 to 2001, a flag with the Confederate flag tucked inside it. The beauty of this flag is that you essentially got two flags in one. The grotesqueness of this flag is the whole "symbol of racism" thing. Note this flag lasted until 2001! There was already Internet, we already tried and tested the Grunge era, parachute pants came and went, my mother had an AOL account, we developed truly nonstick pans, everyone had microwaves, the Olympics games were held in Atlanta for an international audience...and through it all, through it *all*, this was the state flag of Georgia. I mean, 2001!??!

We responded with scattered: "Oh, really? Oh, okay, yeah, totally cool, sweet, yeah, cool, cool, got it, cool..." We finished filming, hopped in the car and immediately Googled "Confederate flag" on every device available until we found out that, yes! This was a Confederate flag! Not "a flag from the collection of eleven states just after the colonial era"—that's way too wordy for a flag! Even a flag from the nineteenth century! Those people had some verbal flourish, but "a flag from the collection of eleven states just after the Colonial era" is like multi-syllabic mouth rape.

NO, SERIOUSLY, THAT CONFEDERATE FLAG JUST WON'T QUIT

Oh, my previous sidebar makes it sound like Georgia was the only case of head-scratching Confederate flag commitment. For any of you who lived through 2015, you'll recall a particularly horrific mass shooting of black parishioners during a Bible study at a historically black church in South Carolina. The shooter had posted photos of himself with a Confederate flag, a website with white supremacist ideology, and other upsetting fare. Then everyone suddenly remembered that the Confederate flag was indeed flying over the state capitol of South Carolina. For a week, politicians of every stripe, including South Carolina's own governor, decried the flag, wanted it taken off public grounds. It even trended on Twitter, so you know it was *important*. But after all of that—the appalling shooting, the endless rhetoric, the nonstop pundits—a CNN poll showed that 57 percent of Americans don't think the flag is a sign of racism. Among Southern whites alone, 75 percent of them don't think it's a sign of racism. Whereas 75 percent of Southern African Americans *do* see it as a sign of racism. So basically, most white people think the flag is like, meh, no big deal, it's a sign of Southern pride, what's the problem? That is probably a problem. Nevertheless, after the national hemming and hawing, both houses of the South Carolina legislature voted to take it down. The governor scheduled the removal for a couple of days later, when the flag would be moved to a museum that probably has a great "hateful things collection." The removal of the flag was, in a word, ceremonial. Or in three words: Cer. E. Monial. Several honor guards in white gloves gingerly handled the flag, making sure that the symbol of racism and bigotry wouldn't get smudged. The flag might have represented a shameful chapter in the nation's history of slavery, but let's make sure none of the fabric runs. On a totally unrelated note, there was no effort made on the issue of gun control. Because the parishioners were shot with flags.

(You can find the stats here: Jennifer Agiesta, "Poll: Majority Sees Confederate Flag as Southern Pride Symbol, Not Racist," *CNN*, http://www.cnn.com/2015/07/02/politics /confederate-flag-poll-racism-southern-pride/.)

What's strange is that he didn't want us to perceive him as a guy who *would* have a Confederate flag. He wanted us to think of him as some kind of erudite historian, keeping civilization alive. But why would you want to keep *this* bit of civilization alive in such a majestic way? I mean, you dedicated an entire field to this flag and the sixty-foot flagpole looks freshly polished. I can understand finding something positive about the region's cultural history from that era and championing that— mint juleps, say, make a big old flag commemorating the fine Southern tradition of mint juleps. But the Confederate flag is so wrought with slavery, legal slavery. Legal slavery that was the underpinning of our nation's Civil War. Which is to say, we almost didn't have a unified country because this one region wanted slavery so bad! What I'm trying to say here is, there are better flags out there.

This little interaction illustrated the extent to which haters live on a spectrum. Hate's bizarre twin, Love, is also on a spectrum that goes from "What a thoughtful text message" to "He's stalking me and I'm so scared." So it stands to reason that Hate would have its strange little

NO REALLY, THE FLAG IS STILL HANGING ON

Oh, my previous two sidebars makes it sound like Georgia and South Carolina were the only cases of head-scratching Confederate flag commitment. Turns out, the Confederate flag is also a part of the Mississippi state flag. They have no plans to remove it.

dimensions and nuances. I have gathered here a taxonomy to explain some of the species in the genus Hate.

FUN FACT: MUSLIMS USED TO BE SLAVES, TOO!

That's right: Just when you thought there was no overlapping theme, just when you thought I really couldn't create that black-Muslim connection that I so yearned for in college, I hit you up with this fun historical fact: some of the early slaves were big ol' Muzzies. Yes, in 1528 a Moroccan Muslim dude named Estevanico ended up in Texas with some Spanish explorers. Did they capture him? Yes! Did they give him a Christian name? You betcha! He ended up escaping captivity and exploring the future southwestern United States. There were other solo guys like this one, but more notably anywhere from 10 to 20 percent of African slaves were Muslim. They were all routinely converted to Christianity, but they got their start in Islam. So in a way, we're just as much a Muslim nation as we are a Christian nation, which is as much as we are a Buddhist nation, or a Jewish nation, or a Zoroastrian nation...because we're not supposed to be an *anything* nation! There's separation of church and state. (Or at least there should be, *amiright*? Who's with me!?)

Swing Haters

The Confederate flag owner above struck me as a "Swing Hater." The Swing Hater is sister to the swing voter, but way worse. If you look at swing voters, they aren't registered Democrats or Republicans. They're usually not black—being black makes you a likely Democrat. And they're usually not Southern evangelicals, because they are usually GOP voters.[1] Above all, they just can't decide!

1. This is according to the all-knowing Nate Silver: "Swing Voters and Elastic States," *FiveThirtyEight* (blog), *New York Times*, May 21, 2012, http://fivethir tyeight.blogs.nytimes.com/2012/05/21/swing-voters-and-elastic-states/.

They're ideological sluts willing to be persuaded from one camp to another. They're totally noncommittal—like the men I've dated—they might call you, they might not call you, it's any pundit's (or suffering woman's) guess.

Like the swing voter in electorally coveted states like Ohio and hanging-chad Florida—the swing hater is on the fence about whether to hate. They can be convinced to hate or not to hate. The swing hater is where I think we can win some big votes. Because this flag man, he really didn't seem to mind that a bunch of minorities were on his property. If we had invited him out to a cup of coffee, he probably would have accepted. He likes *people*. But he was raised with this flag, and frankly, given the geography of where we found him, he wasn't around much diversity. He had a huge blind spot about what the flag meant to nonwhite, non-Southern people. Once that blind spot gets filled with information and exposure, the swing hater turns into a swing lover. (Oh wait, "swing lover" has a totally different connotation, but you know what I'm getting at.)

This kind of thinking rests on the notion that *people can change their minds*. There are those of you who don't think that's possible—I'm looking at you, Curmudgeon McSourpuss. If you think that attitude change isn't possible, then how can you explain gay marriage? The statistics on gay marriage have changed so dramatically that you would think

---

And according to this paper from the Brookings Institution: William G. Mayer, "What Exactly Is a Swing Voter? Definition and Measurement," Brookings Institution, http://www.brookings.edu/~/media/press/books/2008/swingvoterinamericanpolitics/swingvoterinamericanpolitics_chapter.pdf.

Bill O'Reilly has come out of the closet with his lover Glenn Beck, and they're going to ride into the sunset together (right after Glenn draws little hearts on his chalkboard). In 2001, 57 percent of Americans opposed gay marriage, 35 percent supported it, and I suspect that that undisclosed 8 percent were picking their noses and the surveyor didn't want to talk to them.[2] By the time of this writing, 55 percent supported gay marriage and 39 percent opposed it. That's what social scientists call "flipping shit around." That's not just because marriage deniers have died off. Oh no, even when you break down the statistic by age group you find that baby boomers, for example, went from 32 percent supporting gay marriage to 45 percent supporting gay marriage. That's because *people change their minds.*

Evangelicals have gone through the most stunning change on this score. These were the same people who always used the joke that God created Adam and Eve, not Adam and Steve (that felt old even when it was new, if you know what I mean). These were the fire and brimstone people. It seemed like they would never change. And yet, one report shows that their support of gay marriage went from 20 percent in 2003 to 42 percent in 2014.[3] Can you believe it? The evangelicals! E. Van. Gelicals!

The human brain is a big fat neuroplastic video game

2. The picking-nose theory on the undisclosed 8 percent is mine alone. But the other statistics are from the Pew Research Center, where many great statistics are born: Pew Research Center, July 29,2015, http://www.pewforum.org/2015/07/29/graphics-slideshow-changing-attitudes-on-gay-marriage/.
3. Elizabeth Dias, "How Evangelicals Are Changing Their Minds on Gay Marriage," *Time*, January 25, 2015, http://time.com/3669024/evangelicals-gay-marriage/.

with thingamajigs sending boops and beeps to whosa-macallits along various different delivery routes. Those boops sometimes become beeps, and beeps sometimes morph into boops, and right turns become left, and left turns decide to go straight, because the brain was designed to change. What I'm saying is, I'm a neuroscientist and this paragraph is tantamount to going to medical school.[4]

FORGOTTEN OBJECTS OF HATE THROUGH HISTORY

Haters gonna hate but sometimes they neglect people, places, or things worthy of a real fist curl. This is a list that hasn't gotten enough attention in the Annals of Official Hate. They are the B-sides to history's more obviously vile subjects, like Hitler.

☐ Biff from *Back to the Future*

☐ Gossip columnists

☐ Awards show fashion commentators

☐ Exxon

☐ People who sell derivatives

☐ People who brag about their Blu-ray libraries

☐ The recipients of the statement "Why you gotta hate?"

☐ People who describe a movie they just saw in too much detail

☐ The kid who didn't pick Abraham Lincoln for his dodgeball team in second grade

☐ Monsanto

---

4. If there's anything you should have learned by chapter 10 of this book, it's that I'm not a neuroscientist. In fact, that's the one thing I want people to take away from this book: "She's not a neuroscientist."

☐ Flip-flop enthusiasts

☐ Smokers who overgesticulate with lit cigarettes

☐ Workaholics who make everyone look bad even though everyone's normal

☐ People who write listicles (that's me)

☐ The people who started "Gamer Gate"

☐ The people responsible for multiple reboots of a franchise

☐ The guy who invented high heels

Haters 2.0: The Trolls

No hate taxonomy would be complete without looking at the modern-day digital hater. These are your lunatics and assholes, vermin and brutes, monsters and jackoffs, your degenerates and diabolical villains who—under the guise of anonymity—populate the comment section of all Internet sites everywhere.

Like most ethnic ladies, female comedians, females, and humans who have visited the Internet, I have been hated on real hard by this devoted group of virulent misanthropes. My voice and nose have been criticized on YouTube, my jokes have been punished and misunderstood on Twitter, my e-mail has been dumped on with hate mail wishing me to die in various forms, critiquing my lipstick, asking me to change everything about myself. But to be fair, I also get fan mail asking if I wouldn't mind being set up with someone's brother, mail apologizing for the climate of a town I just performed in, and mail just plain old appreciating my work. Of course the fan mail is delightful—who would pretend otherwise?! But the hate mail, that can be as enjoyable as a Pap smear.

Here is a nifty list of some of the comments I've received on the Internet:

- ☐ I watched and you were disgusting.
- ☐ Your video gave my computer cancer.
- ☐ U guys are gay I hate U Americans why are U soooo STUPID gosh have a brain.
- ☐ *In response to a show announcement*: It is not even worth selling for 15$. You Muslims are not even human beings. Looking at your faces at stages won't make anyone laugh. Most people in this world are familiar with your vile and intolerant religion. It is not you Muslims that are violent. It is Islam and Allah itself that are violent. You Muslims should not be allowed to live.

  (For the record, this commenter was really mad about a free show, not a $15 (or as he said, "15$") show.)
- ☐ Hey Dicksucker—did your boyfriend blow his aids infested wad up your butt this weekend, fag?
- ☐ go live in another country, better yet work in State Prison for 10 years and then tell me about how insensitive America has become. The real fact is ISIS is training right now to kill your whole family and shit down your neck hole after they remove your head with a dull blade.

- □ I'm sorry if you suffer from jealousy that you never had what it takes to be a real man.
- □ This is the kind of idiocy that keeps Isis going.
- □ You communist punk.
- □ Stop whining you pansy lip flap.
- □ What an idiots.
- □ Negin farsad your parent did not raise you the right way. you are a bitch.
- □ This cunt would be killed in Afghanistan.
- □ is there anyone who can kill these rats in the comedy show please...i can pay u up to $50.
- □ God her voice sucks and is annoying. My ears are starting to bleed after this shit.
- □ She looks jewish lol but still funny.

Trolls are like the bedbugs of the Internet. They happen, they bite hard and leave an ugly mark, and you get a dog to sniff them out and then kill them. But inevitably they pop up on another side of town. It's a real scourge, and because they can create endless Internet bullhorns (additional fake accounts), their voices get needlessly amplified.

VOICE MAIL HATERS

These guys want all the anonymity of an Internet troll without all that typing. Their whole shtick is to leave voice mails on people's phones. My parents were the recipients of one of these audio gifts from a voice mail hater. At the time, their phone number was listed and because mine isn't, the hater looked up my parents' number. They said something like "We know what your daughter does and she's un-American, and you are, too, and if she keeps doing what she's doing she'll suffer the consequences." Something like that. My dad deleted the voice mail in a fit of anger—I have learned that my parents don't like receiving death threats on my behalf. They also don't like that I receive death threats. I can't say that I'm fond of it, either. Mostly, I would like everyone to leave my parents out of it. They're really nice people. Way nicer than me. Also, I'm a comedian. How is death a proportionate response to not liking my jokes? What if someone breaks your leg? What would your response be to that? Would it also be death? Because, see, it's weird for "not liking jokes" and "broken leg" to merit the same response. A more reasoned response would be not listening to my comedy.

You might think that troller comments matter only to the author being trolled. You might think, Hmmph, it sucks to be them because these comments are HARSH! Never mind the fact that, yes, it does suck to be them, but it turns out you, the comments section reader, are also being affected. The *Journal of Computer-Mediated Communication*—a magazine fancy enough that it is not carried in the supermarket—published a study where they had one group of people read a scientific article without reading the comments, and then a separate group read the same article including the comments. The people who read the comments had a way more polarized view of the contents of the actual article.[5]

Trolls create conflict where there might be none through Twitter wars, exponentially growing comments, and needless back-and-forths. They create multiple identities to send the same hateful message. They make noise where there's no real noise, just one shitty troll being a meanie. That's right, they're *meanies*, and they treat the Internet like it's a schoolyard for their bullying.

When I see a troll, I try not to engage, because if you engage, you escalate. It's like that lame bacteria in your gut that feeds off of sugar. Cut off the sugar and the bacteria dies. It's hard to cut it off, because brownies are delicious. Yelling at an asshole can also be delicious, momentarily. But at the end of the day, it's better to let the thing die off.

The Drive-by Hater

This is where bigotry takes a turn for the lazy. In my travels, I've seen a proliferation of this new generation of bigots: The drive-by haters. I was in Salt Lake City for a show. Salt Lake is the capital of Utah, the most religiously homogenous state of the union, and that religion is Mormonism. As one of the newer religions on the block, the

5. Ashley A. Anderson et al., "The 'Nasty Effect:' Online Incivility and Risk Perceptions of Emerging Technologies," Wiley Online Library, http://onlinelibrary.wiley.com/enhanced/doi/10.1111/jcc4.12009/.

Mormons are maligned. Most of what people know of them are from HBO's *Big Love* and Broadway's *Book of Mormon*. So basically, the Mormons are considered a people who have a lot of wives with whom they break out into choreographed song-and-dance numbers. I'm not saying I'm jealous of this "multiple wives" stereotype, but it does have a gentler ring to it than "terrorist."[6]

Lest we forget, there are Mormon feminists out there who will tell you polygamy is no longer a thing among polite Mormon society but also that the church still denies women the priesthood. Turns out, like all other religions, Mormons aren't without their problems and fissures. But alas, they still shouldn't be so maligned.

But I digress. My point is, I was standing in Salt Lake City in front of the main Mormon Temple with excellent fellow comedians Dean Obeidallah and Kareem Omary, and I was holding a sign that says, HUG A MUSLIM. If you've never stood in front of a Mormon temple soliciting hugs, you haven't stood. Those Mormons brought with them hugs so tender and warm, so loving and mirthful— yeah, exactly that, mirthful—that it warmed the cockles of my heart. My heart cockles were hard, overburdened and scarred with little patches of snow and potholes. But those Mormons, man, each touch smoothed out a piece of scar tissue until my cockles were as smooth as Sofia Vergara's calves.

---

6. Although, to be fair, Muslims also get the "multiple wives" stereotype, but it's usually overshadowed by the "extremist violence" one, so my point still holds.

In the midst of this mirthful display—a display that gave me the weeps and sent our associate producer, Leonard, to literally sob behind a statue of a famous Mormon until he composed himself—in the midst of this display, there was a dude who drove up to the adjacent stoplight, rolled down his window, and when the light turned green, he yelled out his window, "Go back to your own country!" He was driving away as he said it, so I couldn't see what he looked like. It could have been a woman with a very gravelly manvoice. It could have been a fellow Iranian, putting on his best bigotry accent and pulling one over on me—who knows? But I'm pretty sure it was none of those things, it was simply a guy who hates Muslims. What was worse is that he didn't even stop the car! This wasn't the first time this had happened to us. This happened to us in other cities like Tucson and Birmingham—always some guy at a stoplight, summoning his little racist courage, and then saying something horrible as he drives away. These drive-by haters are either cowardly or really busy and have somewhere to be.

Drive-by haters are also the most likely to put a swas-
tika in their dashboard window, bumper stickers that say,
THERE'S A FEMINIST IN MY TRUNK, and the I WANT YOU TO
SPEAK ENGLISH car decals. They want to be racist with
their accessories but might stop short of actually doing
anything about it. It's kind of like teenagers who wear
various punk/anarchy-themed gear but report to geome-
try class on time every day and get good grades.

Drive-by haters are also the most likely to confuse
Sikhs with Muslims. They see a turban and they have
a knee-jerk reaction. In fact a survey showed that about
28 percent of respondents misidentified a Sikh as Middle
Eastern (they're usually Indian).[7] Basically, I wouldn't say
this group is big on research or accuracy.

I will say for the drive-by haters, that at least they're
not as lazy as the online haters. Those guys can clock in
a full day of bigotry without leaving their laptops. Now
that's *lazy*.

The "Mission-Oriented Bigot Whose Group Affiliation Gives Them Cover for Hating" Hater

There is another category: the Organized Mission-Oriented
Bigot Whose Group Affiliation Gives Them Cover for
Hating Hater. It's a working title. These guys have insti-

---

7. Emma Green, "The Trouble with Wearing Turbans in America,"
Atlantic, January 27, 2015, http://www.theatlantic.com/politics/archive
/2015/01/the-trouble-with-wearing-turbans-in-america/384832/.

tutional affiliation—oftentimes a church—that give them some kind of legitimacy (at least in the face of any non-analytical observers). When I was doing a screening of *The Muslims Are Coming!* in Centralia, Washington, I met some of these folks. A small but mighty group of local Christians protested my screening. They held up signs asking people not to see the movie because I was going to try to convert them to Islam. The picketers were in for a rude awakening, because you actually learn very little about Islam from my movie. Spoiler alert: I'm not a Muslim scholar, so the movie is not about religion, it's about cultural acceptance. Plus, I talk about jizz and vaginas throughout the film, so it's more likely to offend evangelical Christians *and* Muslims rather than convert anybody to anything.

I invited the picketers inside to see the movie. It was cold and raining, and I've seen enough *Twilight* movies to know that it's not safe in Washington State once the sun goes down. Alas, they didn't bite. But they did at least stand in the lobby during the screening, because most religions don't want you to get rained on. While I was nice to them, sincerely invited them inside, I didn't push too hard. There's a fine line between making yourself open and available, and offending or proselytizing.

The American Family Association is a well-oiled machine that falls into this category. They have organized radio and television shows that broadcast on regular old cable. Having a media presence shows that you're not so crazy that you can't hold down the responsibilities associated with airwaves and content. The AFA uses this airtime to talk about Jesus and God in a way that sounds very Christian and loving. And then *bam*! They hit you with stuff like:

> The homosexual agenda represents the single greatest modern threat to freedom of religion and conscience.
> —Bryan Fischer, AFA

> There is no spirit of God in Islam. It is the spirit of Satan. It is the spirit of darkness. It is the spirit of tyranny. It is the spirit of bondage.
> —Bryan Fischer, AFA

> Homosexuality gave us Adolph Hitler, and homosexuals in the military gave us the Brown Shirts, the Nazi war machine and six million dead Jews.
> —Bryan Fischer, AFA[8]

That was a fun little Muslim-and-gay sandwich, wasn't it? If they hit you up with a bunch of loving stuff from the church about being saved and God's love, it's easy to squeeze in these little hate nuggets, because the group affiliation provides cover. Hence the "Mission-Oriented Bigot Whose Group Affiliation Gives Them Cover for Hating" Hater.

---

8. "Quotes from the American Family Association," Southern Poverty Law Center, http://www.splcenter.org/get-informed/intelligence -report/browse-all-issues/2011/winter/afa_quotes.

Reform Hater

Then there are people like Gov. George Wallace of Alabama. For those of you who don't know, Wallace was a towering figure of the Civil Rights era but on the wrong side. He said stuff like: "Segregation now, segregation tomorrow, segregation forever!" And after losing his first gubernatorial bid to a *more radical* white supremacist (yeah, he wasn't even the worst guy on the racist spectrum) he said to his aide: "You know why I lost that governor's race? . . . I was outniggered by [the opposition]. And I'll tell you here and now, I will never be outniggered again." George Wallace *hated* black people. He didn't want them to vote, he didn't want them to cross a bridge and march into Montgomery, he didn't want them to use the same doors or the same seating areas as white people. And when everyone else was bobbing their heads to Diana Ross and the Supremes, George Wallace had to forcibly stop his hips from swaying and remind himself that he hated black people. That's commitment.

But what has always fascinated me is that he is probably the most historically storied figure to dump his earlier ideology and admit he was wrong. *Yes.* He did that. In 1972 he survived an assassination attempt that paralyzed him and bound him to a wheelchair. His wife had died a few years prior from cancer, and things were just not going his way. He was still governor of Alabama, mind you—and would serve four terms total; his last nonconsecutive term was in the '80s! But as the story goes, he was in constant pain and he had time to reflect and realize, "Holy shit, racism is horrible." (I'm quoting the inside of his brain.) In his later years, he would go to any black church that would have him and ask for forgiveness.

In 1979, at the Dexter Avenue Baptist Church in Montgomery, he said to all black parishioners: "I have learned what suffering means. In a way that was impossible [before the shooting], I think I can understand something of the pain black people have come to endure. I know I contributed to that pain, and I can only ask your forgiveness." Some were skeptical up until his death in 1998, but others really believed that he turned it around. I for one, would like to think that he evolved, he improved, he found reasonableness.

But when George Wallace was at his prime, he was the kind of old-fashioned bigot that you just don't see anymore. He was rash and loud, he would scream invectives at the top of his lungs, and he was definitely not worried about how he came off in YouTube videos. They really don't make bigots like that anymore.

Other Famous Turnarounds

☐ **Alan Chambers** of Exodus International, the "pray the gay away" operation to turn gay Christians into heterosexual ones so they wouldn't be eternally damned. After twelve years of helming the organization, Chambers admitted the reparative therapy didn't work and that gay Christians didn't need to repent in order to go to heaven. Boom! A turnaround!

☐ **Malcolm X** was a Civil Rights–era heavy hitter. He spent his early years as a member of the Nation of Islam, where he preached that white people were the devil and that black Americans should completely separate from them. Then he went on a hajj—a Muslim pilgrimage to Mecca—came back, and renounced all of his earlier positions on white people. Kablam! A turnaround!

☐ **John Quincy Adams** had a total boner for manifest destiny in his early years; he thought America was destined to expand from coast to coast. But later in life he fiercely resisted expansion, because it meant the expansion of slavery. As a result, he opposed actions—war and otherwise— that would lead to the biggening of the country. Manifest destiny? More like Non-ifest no-way-stiny! Turnaround!

☐ **Bill Maher** Maher was a truly funny comedian who spent many years on his HBO show talking mad shit about Muslims at every opportunity. He made claims like "hundreds of millions of Muslims" supported the *Charlie Hebdo* attacks. Which, is, you know, ludicrous. Then in 2025—which is a date in the future—Bill Maher realized that Muslims are normal people. He remained an avowed atheist but took a more loving approach to Muslims. He and Pope Francis started a new talk show on HBO called *Pope Talk with Bill Maher and a Pope*. Pope Francis, it turns out, does great bits.[9]

---

9. Alas, this is all untrue, as I cannot accurately tell you what will happen in 2025. Or can I?

The taxonomy of hate is useful, because it helps you figure out what kind of haters you're dealing with and whether you should make an attempt at bringing them in the fold, whether they're too far gone to bother with, or whether you're crossing that fine line between reaching out and goading.

I did cross this line once. The goal of *The Muslims Are Coming!* was to make ourselves available to people who were curious about Muslims. To stop them in their tracks in the middle of their daily lives, offer them pastries, and engage. We did this quite effectively by setting up an Ask a Muslim booth in the middle of town squares. People asked us questions, or they hurried by, or they were so intrigued by the free pastries that they stopped for a sweet, and then got roped into conversation. It was fun, it was sometimes difficult, and it was always eye-opening.

We got questions like "If Muslims aren't terrorists, why don't we ever hear them denouncing terrorism?" Sometimes the question was posed as, "We see all these terrorist attacks happening, and I just don't see any Muslims expressing any dissatisfaction, it's almost like they're okay with it or like they kinda want it to happen." Which is a particularly illogical formulation, because if a Middle Eastern immigrant left the Middle East, it's because they wanted to have a more "American" life, right? It's not like you would leave the Middle East if what you want to do is live in a place that will be invaded by "the Middle East."

Illogical or not, it's a legitimate question. And we heard it over and over, which means that people have really *not* heard Muslims denounce terrorism. But that's really strange because the only Muslims I know *do* denounce terrorism. I think the biggest problem is that our mainstream news outlets just aren't going to cover a bunch of reasonable people denouncing violence. Beyoncé's skirt could fly up, or Oprah Winfrey could endorse another book, or Hillary Clinton could say something about hating Spanx when she thought her microphone was off—any of that would be covered *before* nice people saying violence is bad.

Nevertheless, the question is frustrating. It's as if Catholics had to denounce pedophilia every time there was a news story on an abusive priest. They just don't do that, because it's obvious that rank-and-file Catholics are disgusted with these priests. Seventy-one percent of mass shootings in the last thirty years were perpetrated by white males, but we don't have white males denouncing mass murder every time it happens.

We also got questions like "Why aren't you wearing a burka?" Another great question. In the United States, whenever we talk about Muslim ladies, we imagine them as shrouded beings. In some countries in the Middle East, covering is the law, not because of the Koran but because of governmental laws (known as the Hadith) that came after the Koran. In the United States, some ladies want to cover, so they do. Other ladies don't. It's really up to them.

The booth we set up, that type of social justice comedy action, was inviting and warranted. But there were times that my tactics veered away from love and into an area of uncomfortable goading. I didn't want to make a movie that provoked people into looking stupid or forced them into screaming matches. But in one instance, I messed up.

THE DAILY DENOUNCER

Because the "Why don't you denounce terrorism?" question has been so rampant, I launched TheDailyDenouncer.com, a comic strip devoted to denouncing terrorism, every day of the workweek (well, the workweek—denouncing takes weekends off).*

*Content by me, ridiculously great illustrations by Monica Johnson.

We were on our way to Nashville for a show and en route we saw a state fair in full swing. We stopped for some cotton candy and to take a ride that made me want to throw up. After feeling the earth beneath my feet for twenty minutes, we were roaming the grounds when we happened upon a bare-knuckle boxing ring that was nestled in the woods behind the fair. I assumed that bare-knuckle boxing matches attract the kind of people who have very little regard for the skin on their hands. The anti-manicure set, if you will. I had never been to any kind of boxing match (let alone amateur bare-knuckle boxing) and we had the grand idea to offer our comedy services in between matches.

I approached the ticket seller and said, "Hello, we are a kindly band of Muslim comedians who would like to offer our comedy services to your fine affair. No recompense required, of course." I then bowed, holding my gloves in hand like a true gentlewoman.

The ticket seller looked at me quizzically. "Muslim comedians?" he said.

"Yes, we would do stand-up, in between matches, you know, to keep the audience entertained while the boxers grease their hands."

He asked me to wait while he asked his boss. We waited for a few minutes and while I stood there I noticed a set of snarling dogs in the corner. "Hmmph, I did not notice those dogs before," I said to myself. I then took a real good look around and fully came to terms with the type of fan who enjoys—I mean really enjoys—the art of bare-knuckle boxing. It means that you have a particular

comfort level with blood, gashes, and other forms of bod-
ily pain. I noticed men walking around who themselves
looked like they had been beaten up—probably because
they had been beaten up. "Hmmph, this whole room is
into violence in a way that I didn't quite notice before,"
I said to myself.

And just as I was noticing the number of empty Pabst
cans on the floor, the boss man ran out from the back. He
was not wearing a shirt, but to honor the event, he was
wearing a bow tie. He seemed to find a large stick that
had been conveniently set against an adjacent wall, you
know, the way big sticks often are. He grabbed that stick,
charged toward us, and in his finest and most threatening twang, he screamed, "Y'all Muslims better get outta
here."

I believe he said other things afterward but we were
running and dumping in our pants at such a fast rate that
I couldn't quite hear him.

This was not the right approach. You don't goad people
who are ripe for the goading into a moment of cultural
understanding. Wrong setting. A general rule of thumb:
If you see snarling dogs, it's the wrong setting.

CHAPTER 11

White People Love Conferences

First Rule of White People: Never talk about White People. I've broken that rule all over this book, so let's go to the Second Rule of White People: White people love conferences. And not just conferences, but "cons": exhibitions, expos, salons, circles, clubs, and basically anything where they can exercise their right to public assembly. The right to public assembly is like the slut amendment of the Constitution—it gets done everywhere! Amiright?

If you really want to make white people laugh, to effect change, to really get the power shifters where the shiftin' is good, you should go to the conferences where our pale-skinned compatriots hang. There are a few notable ones, like PopTech for the tech tastemakers, the Clinton Global Initiative for the international development nerds, Bonaroo for the fucking music hipster fucks. But at the top of the con hill sits TED—the pièce de résistance of elite conferencing.

TED—which stands for Technology Entertainment

Design—was born out of a need for extremely well-connected folk in Monterey, California, to access really innovative technology…oh, and entertainment…oh wait, there was a third thing, oh right, and design. For far too long, well-connected rich citizens had been denied direct access to really cool stuff. They had to research it on their own or call up several different people and have conversations about what was new and interesting. Frankly, it was labor intensive, involved too many phone calls, and the results were mixed. Sometimes what they thought was cool wasn't actually cool, or what they thought was an innovation was kinda hack, and what they thought was entertainment was just a free foot rub.

So, the WCs (Well Connecteds) outsourced their problems to a conference. Curators took the lead and began whittling down everything into bite-sized talks. These talks often came with elaborate PowerPoint presentations, an *ah ha* moment, an unbelievable demonstration of technology, an admission of something really sad, an admission of something really uplifting, and a standing ovation.

They started outfitting these speakers with those face-microphone thingies, filming their presentations, and putting them online. Henceforth, the TEDTalk phenomenon was born. TEDTalks often go viral so that regular people who can't go to the conference can see the Talk. A lot of these talks are truly awesome. Some of these talks will leave audiences driveling in tears, and others of these talks present metaphorical measurements of dick size.[1]

I love TED. And here's the absolutely crazy thing: I'm actually a TEDFellow. That's right, I am one of those twenty people selected yearly for their upstart genius in various exciting fields like neuroscience, big data, and mine—social justice comedy (an as yet unverifiable "job"). It was a huge honor to be selected, and yet I also found it truly surprising. I spend a fair amount of time finely crafting dick and fart jokes. Sure, the dick and fart repertoire is encased in a larger social justice mission, but still! The other Fellows in my class were like inventing shit that's going to save the planet and whatever.

I shouldn't make assumptions, because it is possible I was selected for my arsenal of material on interna- tional toilets (that's like six minutes of material that will blow your mind...and your bowels). Or maybe it was my boob-based oeuvre? Perhaps it was my pitch-perfect imitation of the little known British woman with two

---

1. This metaphorical measurement of dick size is best evidenced by inven- tor dudes, each of whom claim that their technology apparatus is better than any other dude's technology apparatus.

vaginas? That *was* kind of a game changer. I guess I'll never know.

If you've never been to TED—because like me and/ or most people, you can't afford it—it's a whirlwind! As a TED first-timer, I'm in the best position to tell you all about it because, as my new neuroscientist friend explained to me, my brain is more receptive to the chemical triggers on blah blah blah. They're such fucking nerds.

So You End Up Going to TED

You start off by marveling: marveling at the attendee list, marveling at the free granola bars that came in your gift bag, and marveling at your own capacity for marveling. When you're done marveling, you switch gears into being "inspired." Because guess what? PowerPoint presentations are apparently the building blocks of inspiration. I had no idea, but it's true. And if you haven't felt inspired four times by 3 P.M. on the first day, you're totally doing it wrong. Because TED is about being around inspiring people that have the inspiring ideas worth spreading, in the most inspired-idea-spready, air-conditioned environment.

My first duty as a TED Fellow was to give one of these inspiring talks. The talk before mine happened to be about dead babies. First the audience was crying because babies were dying, then they were crying because this Fellow used some kind of science to save the babies from dying, then people were crying because they got to see pictures of how cute and chubby the once-dying babies had become.[2] Then it was my turn. As a comedian, it was my dream to follow a moving presentation on dead babies with a talk called "How to Make White People Laugh"[3] that has the emotional depth of a radish. That said, I did my best to kill it—the audience, not the babies; the babies are doing *great*.

I was extremely nervous, but thankfully I got some big laughs out of the gate. I think the audience needed to experience the opposite of crying. At the very least I did a

---

2. That TED Fellow was Jane Chen. Look her up. She's brilliant...and tough to follow.
3. READER: Oh wait, was that TEDTalk the premise of this book? ME: Sort of, it did lay the building blocks and I did steal my own title from it. By the way, I'm glad you're paying attention. READER: My pleasure, but I might have to put the book down after this chapter to go to my Pilates class. Don't be offended, though. ME: I totally understand, you gotta keep it tight, grrrl.

good job of de-elevating the TED stage from "remarkably insightful and uplifting" to "I think all of her statistics were fake." When I was done, I felt triumphant for five solid minutes and then went back to vaguely self-hating, my natural state.

Once you're done giving your talk you get to meet all the impressive people at TED, people like millionaires! Millionaires are cool because they always smell good and never have dribble stains on their artfully casual but probably expensive T-shirts. TED millionaires are extra great, because they totally hate famines and they super-detest malaria. Don't get Bill Gates started on it, he'll go on *for hours*.

When you're at TED you run into people like Ben Affleck. He's got a hard-on for some part of the Congo that's currently totally fucked, I might be paraphrasing. Or Bono, who has a similar hard-on for extreme poverty, but he talks about it with an Irish accent. Or Goldie Hawn, who walks around in flowy dresses with wonderment on her face and Salma Hayek pretty much looks like a more gorgeous version of Salma Hayek.

By day three you no longer notice celebrities, you're so hepped up on knowledge that everything is a blur and its just weird experience after weird talk after weird run-in. For example, you're walking toward some really exciting free snacks when you bump into one of the guys who invented Skype. He tells you about artificial intelligence he's developing that will outlast the apocalypse. You wonder if he's as excited by the prospect of complimentary Popchips as you are. Then, you cry at a talk by a North Korean refugee while simultaneously wanting to know where she got her cute dress. You decide to take a piss when you run into a war correspondent in the bathroom. You tell her that you would have been a war correspondent if it wasn't for the "war" part. You run into the lobby and stuff more free snacks into your purse.

Free Snacks and Income Regression Analysis

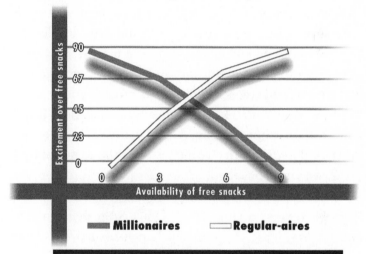

This graph indicates that there is an inverse relationship between level of income & excitement over free snacks. Regular earners are increasingly excited about free snacks as free snacks become more available whereas millionaires become decreasingly excited over free snacks as their presence increases.
-Research conducted by the Schmew Schmeserch Schmenter

You walk by a group of astrobiologists and neuroscientists and you hear them say something something "genome mapping" something "extremophile" something "cyborg cockroach." You remember a spit wad you made in your seventh-grade Earth Sciences class. You see Sergey Brin (a Google founder) and you want to ask him if he secretly thinks his own glasses are really annoying, but you think better of it. You see the fifteen-year old "scientist" who developed a nuclear fusion thing, and you want to ask him if he learned nuclear fusion before or after his testes dropped, but you think better of it (also, you might get arrested). You see more teenaged scientists milling about; one of them invented or maybe destroyed pancreatic cancer. You're mad that these teenagers probably don't care about boy bands, and you decide that they're all old people in young-people masks.

By this point, it's nighttime, and TED has arranged for you to party like a nerd star. Even though you're really tired you go, you drink, you pretend to understand casual conversations about coding. And of course, after the TED Party is the after party (which was *in* the hotel lobby— Jay Z was not consulted). You're desperate for sleep, but you're convinced that Al Gore might show up and do a karaoke version of Journey's "Don't Stop Believin'," so you go, you stay, you notice a bunch of married dudes hitting on girls with PhDs.

The morning of day 4, you're a mess, but you can't sleep in! You can't miss any sessions, because what if Peter Gabriel does a duet with an orangutan or something batshit crazy like that. And then it actually happens: Peter Gabriel does a duet with a fucking orangutan.[4] And then

---

4. Did this really happen? Fuck yeah, it happened. Peter Gabriel does duets with bonobo apes on the regular. Mostly, he wants to figure out how to communicate with them and other cognitive species through technology. He likes to put a piano in front of an ape and then round out the tune with, you now, a Peter Gabriel jam. Look it up!

he and Vint Cerf—who invented the Internet—and a team of kooks reveal that they're inventing the "interspecies Internet" and your brain starts to melt. But then there's a break and…oh thank God, there's free pinkberry!

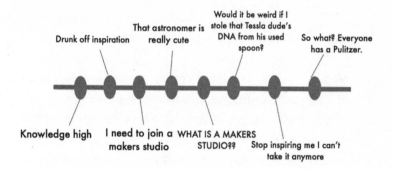

TED IN-CONFERENCE FEELINGS SPECTRUM

And finally, it's the last day. You're ready to weep and feel things at an inspired level for what might be the last time in your life. You try to take it all in while simultaneously calculating how many free protein bars you can stuff in your carry-on bag. There are choirs onstage and images and more talking and more weeping and more inspiration and poof, it's over. And if, by Friday afternoon on the last glorious day of the last glorious TED in Long Beach you haven't set up a 501(c)(3) whose mission is to end world hunger through an interspecies app robot, you obviously missed a session, the one session that would have really fucking inspired you. So fuck you for being so careless, fuck you for missing that session, because now there isn't an interspecies app robot genomic data set to end world hunger! Now who's gonna do it? We can't ask Vint Cerf—he already invented the Internet, can't he take a break? You selfish asshole.

And that is TED.

Hot for Conference: What's the Appeal?

That TEDsperience is basic to every convention only with different details, outfits, and buzzwords. At Burning Man, someone might make a bold and sweeping public statement about EDM and everyone will go apeshit! You're around people who care about the same things that you do. You all get to care about these things in a very loud way. Being around those people adds a layer of encouragement to your convictions, it gives you a boost, the enthusiasm is contagious. It's like the emotional equivalent of someone cupping your balls.

Like my white compatriots, I'm a huge sucker for conferences. One of my favorites is Netroots Nation, where bloggers, journalists, and social justice advocates of every stripe convene to talk smack about the state of the world. Going to that conference makes me feel like I'm an engaged citizen. I learn about how people are fighting the good fight, I learn about congressional races, union fights, environmental challenges, you name it. I'm more engaged in those three days than I am the entire month before it. By my math, those three days make up for like a bunch of months of mild engagement.

Conferences also play into liberal guilt. They're like a

check mark. I paid my dues, I went to this conference, I have the tote bag—now I can go back to thinking about whether the morning barista is hitting on me for the rest of the year! Conferences are great, but they can also be an excuse that keeps people from doing more. I know I've been guilty of that: "Oh, I would march against union busting but...um, I was at Netroots and we talked about it in at least two sessions, so I feel like I've done a lot."

I was at a conference at Sundance, where we watched a Native American ceremony giving thanks to the land. This was definitely our kumbaya moment, and it had all the trappings of a *Portlandia* sketch, but it was genuinely beautiful. For twenty minutes I thought about how the United States government fucked the Native Americans. How they got the worst end of the bargain because so few of them survived the making of this empire. But then... my elbow started to itch. And that was it. But twenty minutes of thoughtfulness is better than no minutes at all.

TED & Burning Man: The Venn Diagram

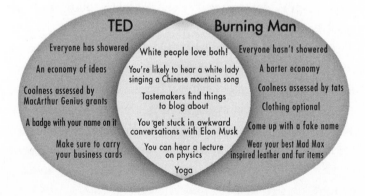

Conferences let you live out your ideology, but just for a week. They let you care in specified weekend jaunts, interrupted only by exchanging business cards and flirting.

This isn't to say that only the lefty feel-good conferences are like that—you could go to PAX (the Penny Arcade gaming expo for people who love video games) and it's the same thing: you might share a kumbaya moment over a really old and ironically placed PacMan. Everyone says to themselves, "Look at us all laughing at blotchy pixels and limited design! I should meet people in person more! I like seeing humans IRL instead of avatars in MMORPGs."

And then three days later you're back in your hometown with headphones on so no one can try to talk to you.

But even events like Burning Man—known for its bohemianism, hedonism, and sunburns—gives people an opportunity for controlled chaos. Your coworker Joe wears a tie all year long, but at Burning Man he wears assless leather chaps. He don't give a shit! He's open and free and ain't no one gonna hold him down. But only for one week. After that week, the assless chaps go back into storage.

Conferences cut both ways. They're great because some real intellectual work gets done. They may also be a superficial way for attendees to just feel better. But then they come around to being great again, because they are such an inviting setting for reaching white people. You don't even need a real in, because you're at the same conference—*that's* your in! Their hearts are open, they can be convinced, moved, seduced, they're wearing assless chaps.

And this is the best state in which to meet white people. So so so many white people. And you stuffed their cards in your free branded tote bag (next to and in between multitudinous free pens and logoed stress balls). You gave them your pitch every time "I do social justice comedy, my current project is blah blah blah, and oh my God isn't it delightful talking to me?"[5] Those white people listened, hopefully they'll remember, and when you need a huge institutional force to support your work, or when you need the dude who invented Skype to invest money in your social justice project that will certainly not make a penny, you have a bunch of cards representing a bunch of white people you met at a conference where you both *felt* things. And maybe, just maybe, when the time is right, you can call on them for the proverbial social justice booty call.[6] In my experience, they'll be up for it.

---

5. Being delightful is a whole separate rule that we will get to later.
6. This is the kind of booty call that doesn't involve any sex but does involve social justice work with a formidable ally.

CHAPTER 12

My Boyfriend Is Black and a Mini-Bout of Racism

I've done a lot of dating. Indeed, countless men have regarded these lady parts and have decided, "Yes, I would like to take this girl out for a sensible meal that does not cost more than $15 a plate and in which she hopefully doesn't order more than one drink, because if I take her back to my place I can get her drunk cheaper on the six-pack of Coors I have in the fridge, unless my asshole roommate drank it, in which case, I'll have to take out the vodka that I hide under my bed." Ah, yes, I've inspired a lot of men into this kind of poetry.

I'm just one heterosexual gal in my own peculiar corner of the dating world. I can't speak for anyone else with any authority, and I have only questionable authority when speaking about myself but, here's my theory: It's hard to date when you're an ethnic lady. Women of color are like day-old sandwiches, you pick one if all the fresh sandwiches are taken. Or, you buy one if you're short on cash and then you're pleasantly surprised when the sandwich still tastes good.[1] When it comes to Iranian-Americans, Indian-Americans, Moroccan-Americans, and what have you, my theory is just a theory. I can't find any hard and fast numbers to prove it. Trust me—I researched like three pages into my Google results. I went deep. Of course part of the premise of this book is that racial and ethnic groupings outside of white, black, Latino, and occasionally Asian get ignored. It's not surprising that I wasn't able to find any real numbers, because again, we get short shrift, even statistically. No regular-sized shrift for us!

But alas, there was plenty of ancillary, extrapolation-y data to support my theory. Take, OkCupid, for example; it's an online dating site that got popular by being free. So if you are really lonely and looking for love in your life, but totally unwilling to spend a dime on your happiness, OkCupid is the site for you! And me, and everyone I've known, because at some point, we have all been cheap fucks dating on OkCupid. It's really great for people who value love as much as they value the free order of cheesy bread that comes with every large pizza order. The Cupes releases various data they've culled from their sad, cheap, and horny community. They'll tell you stuff like "Exactly what to say in a first message"

---

1. By the way, I don't mean to imply that women of color aren't "fresh" as in "not stale"—they totally are fresh. But I also don't mean to imply that they're "fresh" as in "horny." But I also don't mean to imply that they're *not* horny.

where you learn that netspeak like *ur* or *luv* do not get responses at the same rate as *you're* or *love*.[2] So take that additional three milliseconds and type out the extra letters.

But more to the point, OkCupid released data on race. The hard truth is that "82% of non-black men on Ok-Cupid show some bias against black women."[3] Among women, Latinas are the second most penalized group. Conversely Asian women do very well in the online ratings world. So, from this data we can maybe say that Asian ladies enjoy a weird exception—probably owing to some horrible fetishizing and stereotyping of these women as being meek and obedient. And by the way, I have a bunch of Asian lady friends who will crotch-punch anyone who says this to them.

But, generally, if you're a woman of color, dating is *harder*. You're just not as popular even to other minority groups who are in the person-of-color pile *with you*.

I always knew this intuitively, but I was struck with it very clearly in college. Dating in college was a whirl-wind of confusion. As I mentioned, the frat boys decided I wasn't white enough. Although the big get in making out with a frat boy was waking up on sheets stained with

---

2. Christian Rudder, "Exactly What to Say in a First Message," *OkTrends* (blog), OkCupid, September 14, 2009, http://blog.okcupid.com/index.php/online-dating-advice-exactly-what-to-say-in-a-first-message/.

3. Christian Rudder, "Race and Attraction, 2009–2014," *OkTrends* (blog), OkCupid, September 10, 2014, http://blog.okcupid.com/index.php/race-attraction-2009-2014/.

equal parts crusted jizz and peanut butter. So maybe it was okay.

There were the artsy types who believed making out with someone, anyone, was part of the experience of college. They might even write a journal entry or make a collage after a particularly insightful make-out sesh. Sexual experience quickly turned psychological for them. These were the kind of guys who could commit to building a set of origami genitals in their drafting studio, but they might not actually "get in a meaningful relationship" because that would keep them from "experiencing new people" and from "letting my origami collection really explore itself." The free-thinking, hipstery, hippie-y, cooperative-living types on my campus were my bread and butter for an over-the-shirt-bra-still-on boob rub and nothing more.

For these guys, making out with an ethnic girl like myself was a badge of honor. It was the "Look, Ma! No hands!" of sexuality, because it proved just how multicultural everyone was. "I'm so multicultural…" "How multicultural are you???" "I'm so multicultural, I made out with a Persian chick." Then you could up the ante by getting a tribal tattoo.

But between the frat boys and the diametrically opposed hipsters were all the very many men in between. These lads, mostly engineers and/or premed students and occasionally scholars of animal husbandry, were kinda nerdy, kinda cute, kinda nervous, kinda sweet, kinda emotionally shut down. I'm sure they had red-blooded American boners that yearned for the hiking-boot- and performance-fleece-clad ladeez of our wintry campus, but they weren't bold enough to go out and get some.

If the sexually confused co-op bound were an appetizer, these kinda-somethings were my main course in college. They were numerous, they were scared, and they were very grateful for female attention. I somehow met them when they had "just got out of a calculus / organic chemistry / structural engineering" test and were giving themselves a whole night without studying. A few beers in, these boys could almost string together the elements of a conversation with beginner to intermediate levels of flirtation. "Dating" for me in college meant making out with one of them, and then never speaking to them again. I had a healthy attitude toward relationships in college.

I did manage one solid boyfriend in those four years. He was of an Iranian breed I had never met before: an Iranian Jew. Oh yes, for those of you who have never gone to Los Angeles, Jews definitely come in Persian form! It's very exciting because they've got all the Farsi *with* all the Jewish guilt. They love Iran for all of its traditions but would also never live there again because of the historical beef with Israel. He was neurotic, and his all-time favorite filmmaker was Woody Allen, but like the Iranians, his default was gushing and overly earnest poetry. He was equal parts hysteria and quixotic idealist. I think we lasted about a semester.

But be still my little ethnic heart—to this point, I had only known the pleasures of people who couldn't pronounce my name twelve to forty-three times after meeting me. To hold hands in public—and to make it to second and a half base—with someone for whom my entire heritage was understood, that needn't be explained, that was lovely. Of course, as a nice Jewish boy, which in his case trumped being a nice Iranian boy, he would eventually be expected to marry a nice Jewish girl. Marriage wasn't on the table when we were twenty, still somehow knowing this dampened the whole thing. To this day there is something that doesn't sit well when people say, "I would date X-ian person but I wouldn't marry one." It's like a micro separate-but-equal policy that don't smell right. Besides, I've long subscribed to the Dickinsonian notion that "the Heart wants what it wants—or else it does not care." And most hearts don't give a shit about someone's religious background if that heart is also swooning and telling the loins to flare up.

I lost my V at the very old age of nineteen—or to be clear, the last day of my twentieth year, or to be way clearer, the eve of my twentieth birthday. I had a rule, which was that in order to have sex, I had to be older than voting age but younger than twenty. Anything older than twenty, and I would consider myself some kind of spinster handmaiden with an inevitable collection of doilies and a penchant for crocheting. (I hadn't expressed any interest in crocheting or doilies but I knew, deep within, that if I didn't hue very closely to that two-year V-loss window, doilies would emerge, and crocheting needles would miraculously appear in my spontaneously arthritic hands.)

Living in Paris the summer after my freshman year of college, I met the man who would not take but be generously gifted with not the burden but the wonderment of my V. We'll call him Tom. Tom was all Sartre and red wine. He was not remotely French but he was a smarty-pants American from Brown and completely comfortable in his own skin. We spent the summer just chatting our faces off, discovering all the fun things that young college-aged kids on a language-learning program could discover. Mainly that if you drink two bottles of wine, and then eat a piece of bread, it doesn't just "soak up" all the alcohol.

Of course, this story would be too perfect if the V loss happened in Paris—say, in a Left Bank bohemian boardinghouse with a view of the Seine and shabby Rococo velvet furnishings. No, that's not how it went down. You know the old saying, "Meet a guy in Paris, lose your V to him in Boston." That's right, our whole posse of American students from that summer met in Boston for spring break. Boston in March is the pits, but we had free lodging, and all we really needed was a convenience store that sold cheap beer to be happy. The V was erased in a studio apartment, with four of our friends (hopefully) sleeping adjacent to the scene.

I walked around the next day as if I were wearing a scarlet letter *V* on my shirt. I definitely thought there was no way it wasn't totally clear to everyone who saw me that I was no longer a virgin. I thought *for sure* everyone could see it, as if I wore my vagina on my sleeve. The barista would say, "Is whole milk okay?" and I would blush with the red of a thousand roses bursting out of my face—like *She knows! How embarrassing! She knows!*

That feeling stayed with me for a few days. It would be another few years before I dared to have sex again. I kept that shit tucked away for reasons still unknown to me.

But when I graduated and moved to New York, that all changed.

Map of New York by Dating Type

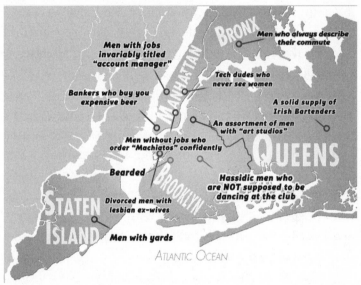

Men with jobs invariably titled "account manager"

Men who always describe their commute

Tech dudes who never see women

Bankers who buy you expensive beer

A solid supply of Irish Bartenders

An assortment of men with "art studios"

Men without jobs who order "Machiatos" confidently

QUEENS

Bearded

Hassidic men who are NOT supposed to be dancing at the club

STATEN ISLAND

Divorced men with lesbian ex-wives

Men with yards

ATLANTIC OCEAN

There are so many men in New York. Tall men, short men, men who lack confidence, men who are overly confident, men who pretend they lost their cell phones, men who are overly in touch with their cell phones, men who send flowers, men who send animated GIFs, men who kick dirt up in your face, men who spend a lot of money on beard grooming, men who put four Splendas in their coffee, men who get a lot of "massages," men who call their mothers every day, men who call their mothers "that bitch," men who refuse to clean the mildew, men who can't even see the mildew, middle-aged men who sleep on futons, twenty-something men who sleep on black leather sofas, men with ear hair trimmers, men with nose hair trimmers, men who use the same trimmer for both, men who deflect or project, men who stick and absorb, men who think it's a jackhammer, men who play it like a dulcimer, men with shaved chests and censure, men with hairy backs and gratitude, and men with nut allergies.

I didn't have a type on my end, but for some reason I managed to only attract white guys and Jews who were in a self-hating phase and/or feud with their mothers. For real. I looked at everyone, I yearned to make hot boning with an Indian dude, but none would look my way. I cast mad booty glances at Asians, but none requited. I looked endlessly upon Latinos and they looked endlessly away. I always found myself chatting with the nearest slightly nerdy white and/or Jewish guy, both anxious about where this bar-side chat would lead.

I wanted to be a cool interracial couple, me an Iranian-American, him a Belgo-Botswanan, or Franco–Sri Lankan or Tajik-Albanian. The possibilities of ethnic mixing were *endless*! This was New York! Surely I could make that happen. And yet, I was always the only one that didn't need sunscreen at the beach. Whenever I was with a white guy and I saw an interracial couple, I had that same feeling you get as when you're in an SUV, you drive up to the stoplight, and the person next to you is in an electric car. And you think to yourself, I get it, you're cool and environmentally conscious and I'm a gas-guzzling trollop riding a dude named Fred. I get it, your dude's wiener is locally sourced and mine jizzes trans fats. I get it.

One night in California, my mom decided to throw a singles party for my brother and my cousins, and I happened to be visiting. I would like to explicitly state the following: (1) I had *nothing* to do with this party, yet I was expected to help my mom clean. (2) My mom is a ridiculous person who somehow gets away with telling a bunch of Iranians twenty-five years her junior that they should come to her house for an Iranian singles party. (3) My cousins and my brother were the in-house team for this horribly embarrassing assemblage. And (4) There were young urban professional Iranians selected from all over Southern California who actually *showed up.*

So, there I was, setting out an array of hors d'oeuvres inspired from some French cookbook but all with an Iranian flare—like a puff pastry with some saffron snuck onto it, or bruschetta that had clearly been spiced up with turmeric, or chicken satay that was made with pomegranate molasses, shit like that. Iranians are incapable of taking a recipe and not Iranifying it. My brother and cousins came over, followed by the swarm of about thirty bonified Iranian singles.

At one point, my mother encouraged me to mix. While stifling a fresh vomit, I walked into the center of the action. A man approached. He made some pleasantries about my mom—yeah, great way to get your flirt on, talk about my mom. And then he asked the most common preflirt question, "What do you do?" I said, "I'm a comedian."

He started laughing hysterically. Oh man, what a knee slapper! He caught his breath, let the wheezing subside, and said "No, seriously, what do you do? Are you like a pharmaceutical rep or something?" I broke it to him gently—I didn't want to invite any more uncontrollable guffaws. "No, really, I'm a comedian." The guy just said, "That's nice." And walked away. Yeah, he just walked away. Because for some Iranians—and maybe even many—being a comedian or anything in the arts is tantamount to being a total slutball.

For these Iranians, putting yourself onstage, making yourself heard, these are not considered "art"; they're considered "exhibitionism." Here's a spectrum from good to bad of what particular Iranians have thought of my profession. Remember, I'm not trying to generalize. This is just my experience, and weirdly my experience takes precedence in this book:

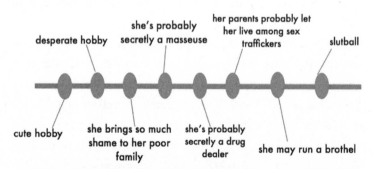

WHAT IRANIANS THINK WHEN THEY HEAR AN IRANIAN GIRL IS A STAND-UP COMEDIAN

*results listed on a scale from tolerably insulting to totally insulting

There was no luck among my people especially the non–Third Thing ones. I needed someone who could understand the Americanness that drives me as well as the Iranianness as well as the love of honey mustard. But I did find lurve in other places. Remember I mentioned that time I had a corporate job? I used to put on business-casual outfits and sit in an office with no windows. It was the kind of office where you got excited for a trip to the bathroom. The kind of office where people made jokes about it almost being Friday.

I stuck out like a sore thumb because I was this Iranian-American girl who, despite the dress code, insisted on bearing cleavage. I was also the only person with comedy gigs at night. I kept this job mainly to use the printer, and everyone seemed to know it. They probably wished they had known it before they hired me for a career-track position in a fancy firm.

I was surrounded by white dudes as far as the eye could see. They were consultant types, loved their frequent-flier miles, and treasured their rental cars. Todd was one of them. But he was somehow more self-aware. We were both based in the New York office but actually met on a business trip in Chicago, where we were instantly drawn to each other. The dude was unnecessarily tall and decently good-looking, but there was a heat wave in Chicago, the jazz bar was bumpin', and we were throwing back the drinks with the zeal of twenty-somethings on an expense account. Because we were twenty-somethings on an expense account. That night, on the walk back to the hotel, as if we were trying to make the night acutely memorable, he decided to show me his swing-dancing moves. We danced on the streets of Chicago, to the music in our heads. Then, after the sidewalk dance party was the after party where, you guessed it, we boned.

Our relationship was immediate, and back in New York we spent almost all of our time together. I avoided using the term *boyfriend*, because comedians can't have cutesy boyfriends and stupid, mushy feelings. I am the type of female comic who refers to my own dick. You can't be in a loving, committed relationship and grab your phantom gonads on stage. It doesn't fly.

I really thought that being in a relationship meant I wouldn't have as much material. I was so worried about being seen as demure or girly that I engaged in a bizarre comedy backlash. I became even more ridiculous on stage. More dudely. More comedian-y. I was scared that love would change my comedy—I overcompensated, I wrote more about jizz and felching. At first Todd used to come to my shows, but I couldn't handle him being there. I wanted him to be in a separate world where I wasn't a girl in love but a crude comedian, all faux-masculine swagger.

We never stopped to analyze our relationship or talk about it, but after a year I started to notice that he didn't call me his *girlfriend*, either. The double standard I had so artfully crafted was now undoing me. In the meantime, I quit the fancy job and decided to go to grad school, preceded by a summer of waiting tables in Paris.

Before I left I started acting weird and grouchy. I was pent up. Todd knew something was wrong, and because I couldn't "talk" about my "feelings" like a normal person, he pried it out of me. He turned off all the lights, drew the shades, got us both naked, and had me turn away from him in the pitch-black darkness, then said, "What's wrong?"

And so I answered, "I'm going to Paris. Is there any reason I should be faithful to you? Are you even my boyfriend?" Todd paused, and then replied, "You know I'm not really into labels, what's the difference what we call ourselves anyway?" And then the horrible, ugly, oh-god-I-have-two-X-chromosomes-and-there's-no-hiding-it truth came out: "The difference is, I love you, and you don't love me."

Silence.

A breakup ensued. In hindsight, we broke up because we were too young to settle down, and because I needed to talk about more cocks onstage. Variety is the essence of cock jokes. To recover from the breakup, I went on a boning spree in Paris (it was more like a make-out spree, if we're being technical). French men are good for this sort of thing. It ended in a couple of solid bits about STD scares and French condoms.

But five years later, Todd was still on my mind. By this point I didn't have a day job anymore. I was doing stand-up, making movies, writing for shows, and generally going through the slog of show business. We talked on occasion and slept together on occasion. But we never got back together until the Great Spilling of Guts.

Like most Great Spilling of Guts, there was a moment of vulnerability—usually a feeling I only allow myself to have if it gets a laugh. We re-declared our love, made a bunch of cheese ball admissions as if we were in an episode of *Gilmore Girls*.

And voilà, we got back together. Now, what I didn't know at the time was that the man I loved was living with another woman, cheated on her with me, just when she thought she was getting a ring. What I didn't know is, in all our backslides over the last five years, he had cheated on many women with me.

When I found out, I decided to overlook it, because I believed in the Negin and Todd Exceptionalism Clause. The one that said being a cheating bastard is morally reprehensible and super hack, unless you're this one magical couple named Negin and Todd, in which case its gonna work out just fine. And we *were* kinda magical, we had bits together! We were going to walk every block in Manhattan! We were gonna paint the walls odd colors! We were totes adorbs!

We were great for two years until he lost his job, became a corporate unemployment statistic, and I became his figurative punching bag. I had no idea how much of his identity was melded into that corporate credit card. Take away a man's corporate credit card and he becomes a surly, barely tolerable eunuch.

He pledged to see a therapist, to crawl out of his anger hole. I was scheduled to go on a tour for a month. When I came back, he was gone. There was no note, he didn't take any of his things from the apartment—he simply disappeared. A disappearance like in a Julia Roberts movie. See what I mean?

I never felt so thoroughly broken. The tears fell uncontrollably, like I was rehearsing for an allergy commercial. And to top it all off, I had to invent my own closure. But my job was still to make people laugh, to tell jokes about Facebook and immigrant parents. I would cry all day long, get to a venue at night, wipe off my face, and tell jokes. My eyeballs would give me ten to fifteen minutes of stage time before they would start spurting again.

"Use the pain," comics would tell me. "Talk about the breakup," they would say.

Once I tried. I told some miserable bit about how, to stop the sadness from the breakup, I had resolved to be a pothead. "Do any of you smoke pot? See I don't because I turn everything into a goal with achievement markers, I would be a really high-strung, competitive pothead…" As I meandered through the bit, my eyeballs couldn't hold out, I burst into tears in front of an audience of twenty-two Manhattanites. Yeah, I'm a professional. I hope you guys enjoyed the show.

But I leaned into the dark rooms we comics inhabit. I leaned into the jokes about dating again. I leaned into the thrill of an unexpected laugh and the thrill of bombing. It was nameless, faceless audiences that got me out of the depression. Audiences who aren't going to disappear unless you really suck. I probably have a horribly deep psychological problem if I need mass audiences to keep me going but…eh, details. Thank God I had them, because that shit was painful. I love you, audience. As for Todd, he just became another cock joke.

What I realized months later—because after a major heartbreak you only sort of realize things months later, you're too foggy and defensive to realize during the relationship or even in the middle of the "sob and pint of ice cream" afternoons—what I realized was that we were doomed from the start. If there was one thing he did to ill effect was ask, "Why do you call yourself Iranian-American? Why don't you just call yourself American?"

When he first asked the question, I shook it off. Todd grew up in Westchester but his mother is from Philly, and so he happily recognizes the Rocky Steps as part of his family's history. Yet, he doesn't accept Tehran's Jamshid- ieh Park as part of mine. But the question became more frequent. Once his shit started to unravel, he criticized so many aspects of my Iranianness. Mainly that I insisted on recognizing my Iranianness. Embodied in him is that thing that some white folk just don't understand. I get this question from people when I'm touring. Why do you insist on calling yourself Iranian-American? As someone once said to me, "If you want to be American, you just gotta be American."

I get it. It's hard to understand why anyone would have a pull to another language or another custom or another religion when the United States gives us everything we need—I mean, hell, every man, woman, and child has access to Pop-Tarts and streaming movies for just $7 a month? America is *great*. But for the eighteen years I lived at home, I spoke an entirely different language every time I walked in the door, I ate different food, I had different rules. Some of those differences I loved, some of them I hated, but they all *existed* in a meaningful way. It might be hard for other people to imagine the indelible mark they left, but I really hope they'll try.

So, love, I learned, has to include not just long walks on the beach at sunset, dutiful delivery of chocolates at socially designated times of the year, and generous foot rubs—although all of those things are 100 percent necessary, of course—but love has got to include me being Iranian, and the man being okay with it.

To find this magical man I went online! Oh yes, I swiped and clicked and messaged my way into many a relationship. I could sniff out assholes from a mere pose in a profile pic; I could go from message to date in less than three exchanges, I could tell just from someone's list of favorite books if he was potentially delightful or a potentially effete snob. Not to brag, but I was good at online dating.

Here's the darkest admission: I like people. I'm what scientists call an extrovert. Even when I went on a date and knew within five minutes that I would never be able to make out with a dude—that I was more sexually attracted to gym socks than I was to this dude, that a life spent in romantic involvement with a Beanie Baby was more realistic than a second date with this guy—I could find something about them that was interesting for the one hour of polite conversation. In fact, I wasn't polite. I pried. I poked. I prodded. "Where did you grow up?

Where did your mom go to school? Did your sister lose her toe in that accident? Was the neighbor professionally good at Ping-Pong or just amateur good? When you say 'poetry challenge,' did you force yourself to write in iambic pentameter or was it more free-flowing? When you first saw your dog hump the furniture, what did you make of it? If your father was still alive today, would you tell him about the poker game where you cheated him?" And so on and so on. I went down every line of inquiry until the person I would never date again left me with a kernel of something interesting. Something I could write about in a book someday.

In this way, I went on a first date with a man who grew up in a cult that he later escaped, a man who grew up on a farm and had social occasion to sit on a bale of hay, a man who built robots, a man who wanted to be a writer but was probably an alcoholic, a man whose shrill voice detailed an even stranger relationship with his mother, a man who grew up in an African war zone, a man who after three years couldn't stop wondering if he had yelled too much at a former student, a man who was by all definitions a star fucker and couldn't stop dishing on C-level celebrities that he dated, and more. Everyone was interesting to me, a few made it to the next round, and I had three pretty solid four- to six-month relationships because: Internet.

But the man that now makes me blush on the regular, that guy I met in real life. Cliché of all clichés, he's an actor, and we met because we have the same acting coach. *Ugh*, I know! It's so totally stupidly show business! We met at our acting coach's annual holiday party, but little did I know that he was on a "celibacy tour," reeling from a breakup that resulted in his pants being bolted shut. His celibacy tour amounted to him going out to various social events but not sleeping with anyone. It would be another year until we actually went on a date.

When it came time for me to tell my parents about this nice young man, I had to break it to them that he was not only an actor—what parent wants their daughter to be with an actor??—but that he was African-American with a smattering of Polish. That's right, suckas! I got my exotic interracial coupling! Of course, my parents, like some immigrants from countries with a homogenous population, gave in to a tiny bout of racism. My mom would say things like "I don't care that he's black, I don't hate black people, I just think your life will be so difficult with a black man." Of course, anyone who has to specify that they "don't hate black people" is standing on very rhetorically sketchy ground. Ground composed of cotton candy and delusion.

But once they met Jason, every last drop of potential bigotry, any mild racism, any doubt about his humanity, all melted away till my parents were puddles of welcoming. (In this case, puddles are very welcoming.) That, my friends, is the power of exposure.

Our gooey DNA will muddy up the American gene pool. That's my mandate to all of you: Go forth and bone, bone someone from across the tracks, across the economic tracks, across the racial and ethnic tracks, across the religious tracks. If you want to make white people laugh, it helps for them to feel sexually sought after in the first place.

Prove OkCupid wrong; defy the statistics, go after the woman of color, and not just the Asian ones. And hyphenated ladies, don't distress, because it turns out that according to another study of that same OkCupid data that "receiving an interracial contact and replying to it makes you send over twice as many new interracial messages in the short-term future than you would have otherwise."[4] That's right, if *you* are an Afghan-American and you reach out to a white guy, he is more than twice as likely to reach out to another Afghan-American in the near future simply because you e-mailed him first! The simple act of reaching out immediately opens up the recipient to new possibilities in interracial dating…and interracial boning. Come on, that's great! High five!

---

4. According to Kevin Lewis of the University of California, San Diego, as quoted in Sharon Jayson, "Online Daters Often Willing to Cross Racial Lines," *USA Today*, November 5, 2013, http://www.usatoday .com/story/news/nation/2013/11/04/online-dating-interracial/3327925/? AID=10709313&PID=6157437&SID=ibtr06tgcg00xkod00dth.

CHAPTER 13

Do Immigrants Spit Out More Patriotic Babies?

After eleventh grade, I went to the Junior Statesmen of America summer school program at Yale. This was summer camp for kids who didn't like fun. It was like a supersized debate team on steroids. It was a program for kids who were capping off their summer not with the beach, but with intense SAT prep. Type A dork-jobs from all over the country would apply to get into this program and the ones who got there—well, we thought we were quite special. And we were, because we were exceptionally uncool.

PhD candidates en route to professor gigs were our teachers and taught us real-deal American history, that is, they went three extra steps beyond your average high school textbook. They even did that thing where they copied pages out of rare books and handed them out as part of our reading. This kind of nontextbook handout seemed very glamorous to me. I pictured elite intellectuals like Albert Camus and Simone de Beauvoir exchanging bits and pieces of obscure French texts with each other, saying things like "Ah yes…" and "This writer understands the essence of being" and "Simone, there's *moutarde* all over this chapter!"

I basically *chose* to spend an entire summer doing *homework*. I was a pretend college student on a fancy Ivy league campus. (The campus was Yale and they would later reject me, but as we established in chapter 2, I'm totally over that and I really don't care and I never think about it anymore, I mean, yes, I've delicately preserved my Yale T-shirt from that summer, but now I have excellent and totally nonenvious friendships with people who went to Yale and any residual bitterness I may have gets siphoned into my YaleWhy DidYouRejectMe.com website, so honestly, I'm fine now.)

My roommate that summer was Kiran, an Indian girl from Orange County, California. Kiran is Jain, from one of those religions where they don't step on bugs (among a bunch of other things; it's a very old religion, so this parenthetical is *not* gonna do it justice—you'll have to pick up a book). I had never met a Jain before, and once I did, I immediately went on to not thinking about it at all. After a week of being at Yale, Kiran and I and my aforementioned Romanian-American bestie Anca (who also came to this summer program) became fast buds. All crushes were immediately divulged to the group, and Morrissey sing-alongs were mandatory.

Kiran and I both had American flags in our rooms back home, so we decided to put one up in our dorm to fill the gaping hole between the minifridge and the Red

Hot Chili Peppers poster. We didn't have a flag on hand, so instead we taped a bunch of pieces of paper together, drew the Stars and Stripes, and posted it on the wall. It was a pastiche DIY flag that would have made Martha Stewart wince. But we felt good about it.

Once it was up, we had Anca, the Romanian immigrant, take a picture of us pledging allegiance to our (basically ugly) flag.

You know, we were that classic American image: Romanian immigrant taking a photo of a Jain Indian girl and her Iranian-American Muslim roommate pledging allegiance to the American flag made of spiral notebook paper. And we really meant that pledge. We were earnest. We were cheesy bastards. But we loved and still love our country like hardcore motherfuckers. Kiran went on to be a lawyer, working as a city attorney for Oakland, California. Anca went on to get an MBA and is now a business owner with fourteen happy tax-paying employees. And of course you know what happened to me, unless you skipped all the way ahead to this sentence.

You know who made these embarrassingly patriotic girls? A bunch of immigrants. Immigrants who fostered a very particular love of country. Correction: They didn't just foster that shit, they *insisted* on it. Immigrants never take this country for granted. They actively think about how fucking awesome it is. They thought about how fucking awesome it was for *years* before they ever even saw the place. That's actually *why they came*. And then they pass that adoration on to their kids. Their kids then make weird paper flags for their dorm-room walls.

Our on-the-margins ethnicities aren't correctly categorized or recognized. Our Americanness is questioned and threatened. Our place in the conversation about race, and the conversation about where we go from here, has never been fully cemented. And yet, we're hardcore flag-making American patriots.

So what do we do?

What I Want from You Already

You've heard me talk about some of the stuff I've done with social justice comedy and maybe those anecdotes have given you some ideas. But here is some more on that front.

Work to Change Your Own Community

If you're a white guy, let's say, you might know a bunch of other white guys. Work to change them. There are those who say, "Be a good ally." For some the word *ally* is fraught, because it implies that we were on an equal footing in the first place, or it implies that we're all in some sort of war. But as a phrase, "person who supports the anti-bigotry cause" has failed to capture the public's linguistic imagination, so let's just say, "Be a good ally." This doesn't mean that you have to go into other communities and tell them what works. Let them, you know, be their own bosses. This isn't *Dangerous Minds*. We don't need a "Michelle Pfeiffer knows best" approach; we just need allies who can work on their own front.

Change That Census

While you're changing your own community, you might run into a guy who can change the census. The census currently has five categories: white, black/African-American, American-Indian/Alaska Native, Asian, Native Hawaiian/other Pacific Islander. That leaves a lot of groups in the lurch. Did you know that the U.S. Census counts people from the Middle East and North Africa as white people?[1] That means a Sudanese-American would have

1. "Race: About," U.S. Census Bureau, http://www.census.gov/topics /population/race/about.html.

to check white. *That's* bananas. And Latinos? They're listed as "Hispanic" under the ethnic origin section but often don't know what to put under the race section. Like would a Mexican-American put "white" under race? How are they supposed to respond?

As a result a lot of us respond as "some other race." In fact, in 2010, "some other race" was the third largest racial group after "white" and "black."[2] But how much information does that convey? It's white, black, and an amorphous group of indescribable people? How can we build policies or have a basic understanding of our country with that?

We have five categories, but why not have 105 categories? Is there any rule that says that more than five categories in the census is gauche? Do we not want to embarrass ourselves in front of other, skinnier census forms? Make a longer census form—who cares! Let us figure out who actually lives in this country, how they identify, and what they need! *Gah!*

Guilt Is Worthless

If you're white, screw white guilt and then go punch liberal guilt in the gut. Don't feel guilt that you were born into some kind of privilege. Guilt is worthless, guilt

---

2. Gene Demby, "On The Census, Who Checks 'Hispanic,' Who Checks 'White,' and Why," *Code Switch* (blog), *NPR*, June 16, 2014, http://www.npr.org/sections/codeswitch/2014/06/16/321819185/on-the-census-who-checks-hispanic-who-checks-white-and-why.

doesn't do anyone any good. Turn that guilt into action. I'm happy that you were born into privilege—maybe I can ride your coattails, maybe some of your good fortune will rub off on me. Mama needs a new pair of espadrilles.

Immigrants, Minorities, Third Things: Stop Getting Mad When People Ask Questions

Do people ask where you're from? That's great! Let 'em know. Don't assume that they're otherizing you. Just let them know: "I grew up in Tallahassee but I'm Indonesian." Why are you upset that someone wants to place you? They've just never seen someone who looks like you, but that doesn't necessarily mean they think you're un-American. Plus, they *should* know where you're from, because in that moment you are the PR for your ethnic group. Yeah, it's unfair; yeah, it's a lot of pressure. But unless you're a real fuckball, why wouldn't your essential you-ness be at least adequate publicity for that group?

And forget publicity; you're a teacher. Yeah, I know, you didn't sign up to be a teacher. But that person didn't sign up to meet a guy named Bojan from Serbia. He's got questions. This might be the only time in his entire life that he can learn about what it's like to be a dude from Serbia. And don't act like you didn't meet a guy from Somaliland last week and have a ton of your own questions for him, too. Questions like, "Where is Somaliland?" Yeah, that's right because even though you're ethnic, you haven't memorized the remapping of the North

African Nile Valley. So why are you upset when someone asks you "Where is Serbia?" or "What is Serbia like?" We all want to understand a thing so we can feel comfortable around it. Be a good member of your community and tell that hypothetical guy what Serbia is like!

Work to Make the News Media Stop Doing the Thing It Does

In early 2015, the offices of the French satirical magazine *Charlie Hebdo* were attacked by terrorists, leaving twelve dead. It was horrific. It was one of those events where you realized why people had to invent the word *horrific* in the first place. Once the news broke, my phone started ringing immediately. News outlets like to get the Muslims on—even if the Muslims they have on are actually experts in other subjects—and they bring them on to make some Muslim sense out of the situation.

In my gut, I thought, Don't take any of these calls. These things do not go well; people are too riled up to think sensibly about what they're asking or saying. But then I thought, If I'm not the voice of a reasonable Middle Eastern–American or Muslim American or Ethnically-Ambiguous-American, will there be others to fill in? We need to have a voice out there, even when being that voice sucks. So I go on a TV show and I was asked if I could terror-splain why the *Charlie Hebdo* cartoons had motivated the attack. I grew up in Southern California, I don't know any terrorists, I'm likely to know more about the history of Capri pants than I am about what a terror-ist is thinking. How could any reasonable person explain what an enema of a terrorist nutjob is *thinking*? (That's basically how I answered without using the word *enema*.)

The show host then asked me this: "Your comic doc-umentary *The Muslims Are Coming!*—how do you feel about it now? Is it the right thing to do?" *Um, yeah!* Building a bridge between American Muslims and the mainstream? Of course it was the right thing to do. Abso-lutely. Totally. Completely. Either the host didn't know the purpose of my work or he just had a knee-jerk reac-tion. A knee-jerk reaction that said, "Anything that shows Muslims in a positive light is insensitive to victims of terrorism." And yet, most people would agree that the vast majority of Muslims have nothing to do with ter-rorism, so we should be able to show them in a positive light because we should be able to show regular people in a positive light. So why did I get a question like that? Why do I have to do so much terror-splaining?

So, can the media stop doing this type of thing? Can you bring Muslims on even when there's no terrorist activity? Can you stop asking us to explain or defend the actions of a few?

In fact, it's not just that we need to stop asking peo-ple to defend their communities against the actions of a few, it's that we also need to stop…covering the actions of a few. Research from Prof. Christopher Bail at the University of Michigan took all the press releases about Muslim stuff from 2001 to 2008, tracked them through all of the Internet, and figured out that "organizations with negative messages about Muslims captivated the mass media."[3] He found that journalists were far more likely to run a story that was fringe and negative than one that was more representative of the population and positive. The corresponding "fringe effect," as Bail calls it, elevates fringe voices to something that is later considered mainstream.

We've seen this time and again. In 2010 the Reverend Terry Jones pledged to burn Korans in Gainesville, Florida. He ultimately abandoned the burning but in the interim he got ridiculously saturated media attention the likes of which would have made a reality TV star salivate. And yet, Jones was a very fringe character with a flock of only thirty people and patchy support. His church was in dire straits. Eventually they moved because attendance wasn't so hot. Covering Jones like he's the leader of a legitimate movement makes it seem like burning the Koran is a thing. Everyone in the United States wants to do it! It makes Muslims feel shitty because they're like "Uh, we didn't know you guys hated us that much." It sends a message to the rest of the world like "Yo, Americans be crazy, they're just out there burning shit!" This whole thing fans the flames of a perceived conflict where there was none. Except now, as the fringe effect suggests, it seems like there is one. We willed it into being by covering it so maniacally. What good does that do?

---

3. "Study Shows Increase in Negative Messages About Muslims in the Media," University of North Carolina at Chapel Hill, College of Arts and Sciences, http://college.unc.edu/2012/11/29/bailstudy/.

Work to Make Hollywood Stop Doing the Thing It Does

I use the term *Hollywood* here for all fictionalized film and television. A few months after I first started auditioning in New York, I auditioned to play the part of a woman clapping in the background at a casino table. I got a callback for that audition because, not to brag, but I'm really good at standing in the background and clapping. At the callback the casting director said "Negin, I think you're really great but you're too ethnic for this part. And if we went that way, you're not ethnic enough." Read: I'm not white enough, I'm not brown enough. I told her that I had some bronzer in my purse, I could come back in more convincing brown-face if that would do the trick.

I've lost out on jobs because "we already have an Arab in the cast." They say that, even when the Arab person and I aren't even from the same continent. It's like saying, "Oh, sorry, we can't have another Canadian in the cast because we already have someone from Bolivia."

I sometimes ask, how would me being Iranian-American and that other person being Arab-American have anything to do with your casting decision? And they say, "Well, you know." And I do know. There's some weird unwritten rule that you can't have more than one brown person per show. There's also an unwritten rule that you can't have more than one "other" in the cast. Like there's either one Korean-American or one Indian-American; we can't handle both. (Unless one of them is passing for white.)

So, let's change those rules! Abolish them immediately!

Is Hollywood worried that if there's one too many Third Thing–Americans in the cast, the audience will just lose its mind? In the latest Hollywood Diversity report they found that only 11 percent of lead roles went to minorities.[4] Would all of television break if that number were closer to 40 percent? Would there just be busted sets all over America if we changed that? The clear answer is no. In fact, another study found that "more viewers were drawn to shows with ethnically diverse lead cast members and writers, while shows reflecting less diversity in their credits attracted smaller audiences."[5] You could be earning more money if you had a more diverse cast. So, abolish the weird unwritten rules!!

The T-Word

This one goes out to the media, the government, organizations, and any individuals out there who have found themselves using the word *terrorism*. Terrorism has become synonymous with Muslims. It's gener-

---

4. Kate Lyons, "Why Hollywood Is Frozen in the 1950s: White Men Are Still King of the Silver Screen with Lead Roles Going to Just 26% of Women and 11% of Minorities," *Daily Mail.com*, February 20, 2014, http://www.dailymail.co.uk/news/article-2563561/Hollywood -place-white-men-New-study-finds-women-minorities-dramatically -underrepresented-films-television.html.

5. Cynthia Lee, "Study Finds TV Shows with Ethnically Diverse Casts, Writers Have Higher Ratings," UCLA Newsroom, October 8, 2013, http://news room.ucla.edu/releases/study-finds-that-tv-shows-with-248757.

ally defined as an ideologically motivated attack on a civilian target. We have so many acts of domestic terror that are not conducted by Muslims, and yet they have all the telltale signs of terrorism. Take Jerad and Amanda Miller, for example—they killed a couple of police officers in Nevada, draping them in swastikas and the Tea Party's "Don't Tread on Me" flag.[6] They then went to a Walmart and killed another lady. This sounds terrorizing, they clearly left symbols of political motivation, and yet the crime? Yeah, it wasn't called terrorism. (And their religion was not disclosed in most of the reporting.)

However, when a man by the name of Muhammad Youssef Abdulazeez brutally shot four marines in Chattanooga in 2015, it was immediately declared a possible terrorist attack (and, yes, his religion was disclosed).

Either all politically motivated violent acts are called terrorism or none of them are. It is hands-down the strangest form of white privilege for mass murderers who are white not to get the "terrorist" label. *The strangest.* We're so committed to maintaining white privilege that even murderers have a better go of it.

So if you or anyone you know uses the word *terrorism*, then let's just dole that out equally. We need to break that linkage between Muslims and terrorism, and maybe

---

6. Paul Farhi, "In the News Media, Are Muslims the Only 'Terrorists'?" *Washington Post*, June 10, 2014, http://www.washingtonpost.com/life style/style/in-the-news-media-are-muslims-the-only-terrorists/2014/06/10 /9ee01778-f0d9-11e3-9ebc-2ee6f81ed217_story.html.

this is one way to do it. The T-word doesn't address all my hyphenated peeps, but remember, turn the dial one degree, and this could be the Jewish people or the Zoroastrians or any number of groups.

Create Something

Throughout this book you have heard me talk about various projects. Well, now I'm asking you to get on that train! Making stuff is fun. Taking people to task can also be fun.

If you see a bigoted billboard, don't get mad. Don't wave your fist in the air. Don't knock your head against the steering wheel. Instead, take a billboard out yourself correcting that billboard in a delightful way. Sure it's hard to raise money, sure it's not going to be easy, but it's better than gnashing your teeth and whizzing by on your moped. Put on plays, write a song, make a crossword, make balloon animals, answer questions in glitter, make art, make jokes, make papier-mâché symbols of community. The opportunities are endless, and it beats sitting home, alone and angry.

If you're not so artsy, how about: Don't vote for racist people, put immigrant-welcoming signs in your window, tutor underprivileged kids, e-mail every major studio and ask for shows and films with more diversity in their programming, listen to your neighbors, then listen to the neighbors across town, set up an "Exchange Your Confederate Flag–Themed Accessories for Cupcakes" stand in your city, travel, learn, hug people, give them the benefit of the doubt, give them your patience.

Expose Yourself (Come On, Not Like That) (A Little Like That)

When kids are born, their eyeballs open to reveal a fuzzy world of hues and confusion. There are no races or sects, divisions or hierarchies, affiliations or classes, there are only vague blotches. How do we go back to the uniformity of those vague blotches?

Exposure is the Triple Crown winningest gold-standard trophy of the cross-cultural games. Exposure means that instead of hating the thing you don't know, you can meet the thing you were supposed to hate. It means information, it means an alternate view, it means a willingness for nuance, it means an emphasis on specificity, it means there is a way to turn things around.

I saw this up close and personal with my own parents. As I've mentioned, they've had a funny way of embracing multiculturalism. They *are* the multiculturalism in many settings, and yet they couldn't quite build a bridge with other minority groups—and they are *not* the only immigrants with this problem. Minorities love to hate on each other—it's the divide and conquer of the lesser classes that has kept the status quo churning.

So here are these people, my parents, both loving, both dedicated to serving their families. My father saves multiple lives *a day*, and he's really, really good at it, better than McDreamy *and* McSteamy. My mother is an outsized unit of support, a caregiver that has been the reason why so many friends and family have succeeded in life! But, for how wonderful they both are, they were always a little weird about Jewish peeps. Dumb, right? Totally counterproductive, right? One day a really warmhearted Jewish couple moved into a house a few doors down from my parents in Palm Springs, California. They showed up at my parents' door with a rum cake. Was the rum cake delicious? *Yes!* Was it made from the blood of Christian babies? I never did get the recipe. But the effect it had was so thoroughly softening that by the following week my parents were besties with them. My mom was calling me to say things like "Did you know that Jewish family is very much like Iranian family?" Yes, lady! Every family is like every family! "Did you know that Jews are very funny? Did you know they have very delicious soup? Did you know they don't eat pork just like we don't eat pork?" *Yes*, lady, *yes. Gah!* They fell so hard, they had me marrying a Jew and making a bunch of half-Jewish, half-Muz babies.

And I thought, Holy shit, all they needed to turn this thing around was a good rum cake? Yes. That was all they needed. They needed to meet the neighbor instead of quietly seething about a neighbor they never talked to. Thanks to the effort of those new neighbors, the tough job of leaving your comfort zone, baking a cake, and knocking on a door—not realizing what you were going to find on the other side—made all the difference.

So basically, always bring pastries. They soften people just like laughs (and they also slightly fatten people). Clearly our international diplomats haven't been offering enough pastries.

I don't even have to look that far to find another example. When I was in high school, like everyone around me, I dutifully bowed to peer pressure and adopted a homophobic stance. I would tell people "Don't be gay," or an object could be "oh my God, so gay," or you would hear me respond with clever retorts like "Duh, of course, I watch *Dr. Quinn, Medicine Woman*, what am I, gay?" Friends and I would have seemingly endless "liberal" views, and then it would come to homosexuality and we would immediately be like "Ew! Gross!"

And then I went to college. One of my first most meaningful comedy colleagues was a gay man. One of my first most meaningful college buddies was a gay man. Dave in comedy land and Jeff in dormland de-homophobicized me to an unrecognizable degree. Together we had so much fun! We got so drunk! We shared expert sing-alongs, endlessly ridiculous examinations of pop culture, curly fries at the student union, and love. I became a double major in theatre (and government) and more members of the gay community came flooding my way. *These* were my people, I thought. I was a fruitfly and I didn't even know it!

I came out on the other side because of exposure. The tough thing about the U.S. of A. is that our geography is based on cars and distance. We treasure space and privacy. We want big lawns and open vistas. We want the fierce independence of the early settlers and we don't need no help! But human beings need human beings. So our open spaces and our suburban sprawl make it so much harder to make those connections. To expose yourself (as in nudity but also as in) to the people and places that will make you an open person.

The Europeans have it easy. Their cities are like a jillion years old and they're built around how far people could hobble on their broken ankles carrying a vat of water they got from a creek. Basically, things are close and more clustered. New York City has that advantage, too; whether you like it or not, you're going to hear umpteen languages and see diversity like it's the front page of a college brochure. And that's just on your way to work. It's easier to run into someone you wouldn't normally meet in places like this.

But for the rest of us, the meet-up is harder. It requires more effort. But one thing a good social justice comedian does is make that effort. It's hard, it triggers some social anxiety, and it makes my palms sweat and my face fire up. But it's a chance to turn things around.

With the spread of American cities, the "freedom" we get with our devices, and the competitive hours of seemingly endless labor, we have all but forgotten our neighbors, our bowling teams, our card games, and our creative salons. There's no more dinner at Ma's house once a week, so the kids can see their Nana because Nana now lives in California and you're in Detroit. The kindly neighbor Phyllis next door can't watch the kids if you guys go out, because Phyllis is the CEO of a Fortune 500 company and the paradigm has changed.

In this new paradigm we learn that "this kinda world don't care if you're home so you better get some." Did I just quote a 311 lyric? Hell yes I did. And I'll quote them or the Butthole Surfers whenever I want! A simple, stupid lyric that swirled around in my head and reminded me always that I can't expect the world to do something, I have to go get it, and more importantly, I have to go change it. I can't complain and kvetch, gripe and grumble. I got to go and get some. Granted, 311 was probably talking about sex, though I've based my existence on this other reading.

In college, I titled an essay, "The Revolution Will Be Served with French Fries." I'm not sure what that essay was about, but somehow the sentiment holds today. There are no blood and guts in my revolution. It will be served with French fries and your choice of dipping sauces— because it's more of a Belgian frites situation—and you will enjoy its greasy goodness!

Your mission, should you choose to accept it, is to go out and serve these fries. If the big actions are too much—like petitioning places that always call security or going on stage and telling jokes for which some nutjob will threaten to kill you—then simply *meeting people* is the microrevolution that is your mission.

I refuse to believe that you're not a part of what's going to make this country better. I mean, come on! *You!?* You're a handsome devil, a smooth and stylish heartbreaker. How could you doubt your place in changing the world? I'm charmed by the very thought of you. Because you're human.

Acknowledgments

Writing a book is a ridiculous privilege. That said, oh my god it's also soooo hard! Did you know? It's like really, really hard. I'm not gonna lie, I had a couple of moments that could best be described as *The Shining*. As in, I was talking to a character portrayed by my index finger. But to keep me sane and to make this entire enterprise possible, I amassed a veritable army of smart people who helped me...constantly. And I shall acknowledge them here, as this is the acknowledgment section.

First off, I always dreamt of writing a book but I didn't dare utter such an absurdly highfalutin' thought out loud until the inimitable, upstanding and charming Daniel Kirschen from ICM looked me straight in the eyeballs and said "You have a book in you." Oh Dan! You were right and you were the OG of this entire book writing venture. THANK YOU, dude. My editor, Libby Burton, gave this book its legs. She had a spidey-sense for everything I was trying to say and sometimes couldn't. She talked me down ledges, or up trees or into creeks, wherever the writing was good, she talked me into that. She is, as the kids say, totally dope. I also have to thank the lovely Sarah Weiss who saw the seedlings of a book and took a chance. Josh Sandler is a dude who gets it, who always has my back, and kicks some legal ass!

"I really have to thank the super cool Monica Johnson whose sure-handed artfulness made the wonderful illustrations in this book. And of course, my delightful long-time colleague and pay Shaddei May Guillaume for her astounding abilities in the world of fake graph generation."

I gotta thank the many many friends who looked at these pages and gave me notes. I aspire to be as sharp and insightful as Jeff Caltabiano, Lara Nahas, and Daria Vaisman. Geoff Kirsch is the kind of guy you meet in a college sketch comedy troupe and then hold on to for the rest of your life because brilliant writers are hard to come by! Thanks to Laurel Brightman because who wouldn't want to get notes from a bestselling writer who *also* wears cute skirts?? Claudia Cogan has an eye for jokes because she is a comedian among mere stand-ups. Rachel Young is one of those cross genre note-givers that I've bothered for nearly every project because her critical thinking skills are like *woah*. Mindy Raf doles out her wisdom with a side of gluten free cupcakes and a metric ton of punch lines. Andrew Mendelson, Lee Camp, and Dean Obeidallah have fought the good fight with me so many times (many of which are described in these pages) because they're better citizens than the rest of us.

Big ups to Andrew Solomon—he told me I should write

this thing at a writer's retreat and then made it happen. Jason Reich also made it happen because he cares and he's funny and sometimes we write movies together. Justin Krebs didn't want to see me languish, nuh huh! And despite having the fullest of heavy plates, he has always made time. Christine Coulson at The Met gave me the stage time to work out the ideas—she runs shit with stilettos on because she embodies cool. And special thanks to the Metropolitan Museum of Art for supplying so many images and making them available to the public.

I have to throw a big warm hug, complete with a blanket and those warming packs that people put in their coat pockets, to the entire TEDFellows team. You really don't know what a *fellowship* means, what genuine institutional support feels like, until you meet people like Tom Reilly, Chris Anderson, Shoham Arad, Patrick D'arcy, Samantha Kelly, Katrina Conanan, and the many others at TED.

Places! Oh places, you were so great in giving me a desk, a view, and some external noise: Yaddo was perhaps the most gorgeous place I've ever written anything while also being extremely well fed. Bryant Park has outlets, people, it has outlets because NYC has still got it! Café Orlin, Spiegal, and the Housing Works Project Bookstore gave me a comfy spot and some hot people to look at when I was thinking.

Kasumi Parker showed me that you could write a book and not fall apart. People like Anca Caliman, Kiran Jain, Arvind Jayaram, Leonard De La Cruz, Steven Synstelien, Mike Dawsen, and Jake Wolff gave me the moments that make a life. Jason Tottenham has been there to pick up the pieces or dance or sing or order pizza or sit quietly and always with love. To my brother and my parents, to whom I already dedicated this book, I wish for your sake I had gone into one of the two acceptable Iranian careers (doctor or engineer) but I thank you so, so much for letting me be a comedian and then building an unbreakable support system around that crazy decision. When I think of you, I know that the American dream is alive and well. Now let's eat some pie.

About the Author

NEGIN FARSAD is an American comedian, actor, writer, and filmmaker of Iranian descent based in New York City. Like most comedians, she has a Master's Degree in African-American Studies. She was named one of the 53 Funniest Women by the *Huffington Post*, one of 10 Feminist Comedians to Watch by *Paper Magazine*, and was selected as a TEDFellow for her work in social justice comedy. She has written for/appeared on Comedy Central, MTV, PBS, IFC, Nickelodeon, and others. She is director/producer of the feature films *Nerdcore Rising* starring Weird Al Yankovic and *The Muslims Are Coming!* starring Jon Stewart, David Cross, and Lewis Black (both available on Netflix). Her next film *3rd Street Blackout*, starring Janeane Garofalo and Ed Weeks will be released in 2016.